MW01611548

HEALING WISDOM

101 Spiritual Truths for Healing Your Illness

The Spiritual Strengths Healing Plan

Richard P. Johnson, Ph.D.

ISBN 978-0-9895130-2-9

10 9 8 7 6 5 4 3 2 1

First Edition

Cover design by Megan Irwin

Edited by Maggie Singleton

Printed in the United States of America

This book is dedicated to the memory of:

Sr. Helene Lentz, CSJ
1947-2011

A valiant champion of social justice of all stripes

An enlightened amalgamator of human energy in the cause of goodness

A star validator of human dignity

Cancer took her too soon.

Books in the Spiritual Strengths Healing Series

by Richard P. Johnson

- God Give Me Strength! Finding the Inner Power to Turn Your Illness/Brokenness/Life Transition Around

- Discover Your Spiritual Strengths: Find Health, Healing, and Happiness (flagship book of the Spiritual Strengths Healing Plan)

- Body, Mind, Spirit: Tapping the Healing Power Within

- Prayers for Spiritual Strength: Physical Illnesses, Emotional Broken Places, and/or Spiritual Dis-eases

- The Ten Most Effective Self-Care Healing Techniques: What You Can Do to Maximize Your Healing Journey

- The Power of Smiling: Using Positive Psychology for Optimal Health & Healing

- Healing Wisdom: 101 Spiritual Truths for Healing Your Illness

- Healing and Depression: Finding Peace in the Midst of Transition, Turmoil, or Illness

- Staying Spiritually Centered for Optimal Healing: Even When You're Sick or Life Seems Out of Control

- Seeking Significance: How to Discover New Self-Direction and New Life-Purpose Beyond Your (Unwanted) Life Transition

Caregiving Titles

- Caregiving from Your Spiritual Strengths: The Ten Fundamental Principles for Optimal Success

- Because I Care...Inspiration for Caregiving for Spouses, Health Care Personnel, Family & Friends

The Spiritual Strengths Healing Plan

The Spiritual Strengths Healing Plan allows you to harness your internal healing power! It is not "faith healing" in which one relies on divine intervention as the sole means for physical cure, nor does it promise cure. Its purpose is healing and is best seen as a supplement to and support for current medical practices. The Spiritual Strengths Healing Plan's philosophy holds that each individual needs to seek the best and most appropriate medical and psychological care they can, in accord with their own personal wishes, and supplement their care with this Plan.

Please note that you will see the word "illness" throughout this book in its broadest sense and may indicate any (or a combination) of the following:

I. Physical Sicknesses

Cancer, heart disease, MS, Lupus, migraine, addictions, hypochondriasis, pain, weight management/loss, smoking cessation, pneumonia, COPD, hypertension, arthritis, immune disorders, Parkinson's, diabetes, stroke, chronic fatigue etc., etc.

II. Psychological Issues

Anxiety, depression, personality disorders, OCD, manipulation, stress, bi-polar disorder, etc., etc.

III. Emotional Issues

Being unrealistic, lacking responsibility, low-self-esteem, career focus issues, poor organization skills, family disharmony, anger management, fears, perfectionism, marriage discontent, lifelessness, infidelity, irritability, chronic lateness, caregiving, etc., etc.

IV. Spiritual Dis-eases

Peace of mind and heart, un-forgiveness, existential angst, inner pain, grudges, scrupulosity, incomplete developmental transitions, guilt, grief and unresolved grief, regrets, blame, disappointments, so-called "unfinished business," resentments, etc., etc.

V. Spiritual Direction & Growth

Gaining better clarity of God's plan in your life, and breaking through barriers that may be hindering your faith journey.

Where do <u>you</u> need healing?

For more information about the Spiritual Strengths Healing Plan, log on to…

www.SpiritualStrengthsHealing.com

The Spiritual Strengths Healing Institute

Learning the art of healing for self and others

Contents

Introduction

This book is dedicated to seeing any illness (be it physical sickness, emotional or psychological issues, or to re-invigorate your spiritual direction or growth) as a master teacher, perhaps even as <u>the</u> master teacher in your life right now. This book does not attempt to sugarcoat illness; its only purpose is to help you see it from a different angle—a vantage point quite unique and yet rich in its ability to show you something entirely new about your illness and about yourself. Whether your diagnosis was recent or remote or whether you're a family member, loved one, friend, or even acquaintance of a person with an illness of any sort...this book is for you.

If your illness is a teacher, then what is its curriculum? What exactly is it supposed to teach you? This is the question that captured my mind and soul; and it's this question that provided the impetus for me to write this book. Ever since I was diagnosed with prostate cancer, I've undertaken a personal study of my psyche...what was I learning from my illness?

I've spent over 30 years as a professional counselor. I've listened to more people than I could count. Each of these folks taught me something, some unique wisdom about the human condition. Counseling continues to be a dramatic learning process for me. Counseling has provided me the foundation to be able to write this book, which is a collection of what I've learned so far about life, the real life beyond our daily routines that instructs us as to the meaning of what life is all about. That's what a master teacher's curriculum is about...discovering what life is all about, and that's what this book attempts to share.

We generally think of a teacher as a beneficent life-enhancer, a mentor who shows the way, a wisdom figure, even a sage or patriarch who gives from the heart and speaks gently of good things. Somehow the rude intruder of illness doesn't easily find company in such an altruistic assemblage as this. Yet, we've all had teachers who may not fit this mold of goodness. For example, I could count neither my high school chemistry teacher, nor my fifth grade teacher in the ranks of the beneficent. On the contrary, they seemed sharp, prickly, demanding, critical, and decidedly non-compassionate. Nonetheless, I remember those two as very effective; indeed, I remember more about them than I do many of the others. Why? They were hard teachers, and they made me pay attention—the same way my illness makes me pay attention!

Just for a moment, consider the possibility that you're only seeing one side of your current illness. In this new light, might your illness actually be a sheep in wolf's clothing? Without question, your illness can be a grim reaper; it saunters through the files of the living randomly picking victims to torment, and worse. Yet, while the venom of your illness is blind to the havoc it generates, it is in a sense a passive victim of its own treachery in that it is also blind to the potential internal personal and spiritual triumphs that its "chosen ones" achieve because of the trials it perpetrates.

Illness takes things from me. Besides taking my time, my mental security, and my painless living, illness can also steal my humor, my sense of order and life symmetry, my peace of mind and heart, as well as my poise and countenance. Illness contorts me; it perverts me, and it drives me away from my counterpoint of balance. All of this and more I count among the losses that illness foists upon me. Yet, under the scattered chaos of the surface of these losses awaits wisdom of great value.

When I dig into my perceived losses, I'm often rewarded with unexpected treasure. Here are some examples. 1) Many people have lamented the loss of a job; only to rejoice later when they realized that the new one they landed was so much better. 2) I remember how forlorn I felt the day I was sworn into the U.S. Army, yet as I look back now, I see what I thought was a loss then as a life gain. 3) We're all getting older, and age demands that we gradually give up our youth. Accepting these losses that are felt like stones in our hearts may actually lay a foundation for a new life stage that ushers in new opportunities for growth and development unavailable before we addressed the losses.

Illness, while maligned as the agent of death, can paradoxically become the angel of light when you come to value the gifts just under its cruel surface. And what might be illness's gifts? Consider the gift of hope. When despair threatens to overpower you, by what force might despair eventually become hope? Illness has a way of taking hold of your life and transforming complexity into simplicity...you focus your attention almost entirely on your illness. This can free emotions formerly blocked and/or overlooked. It allows you to recognize kindnesses that were always there but only seldom seen. It gives you the strength to convert contention into acceptance, and it can transform thoughts of criticism into affirmation. Yes, illness can be a master teacher, and even more, illness can be the alchemist who changes base human elements into interactive and intra-active gold.

Illness, and all severe sicknesses in general, is not the only master teacher of life that offers a curriculum of transformation. There are several others. Aging, the process of true maturation, runs a close second to illness in offering a panoramic new perspective on the real purpose of living. Most of what I discuss here in relation to illness might also be ascribed to aging. And let us not forget the subject of song, sonnet, and untold sentiment...relationships. Traversing the meandering, rocky, and sometimes emotionally treacherous road of deepening relationship is the third "master teacher" of the gems of living. What life lessons have your relationships taught?

101 Truths

In this book I itemize and describe 101 truths (wisdoms) about illness that I have learned in my illness journey thus far. I can't claim these 101 as originating from my own making because I believe that they came from the Spirit. But I offer them to you freely as they have been given to me freely. You may not learn all 101 teachings; some you'll learn better than others, some you'll forget, others may never really penetrate deep enough to grab hold of your attention. But, there may be several that will burst through whatever walls—made of whatever materials you use to protect yourself—and take up residence in your heart and mind. Once there, they'll begin to spread influence over more and more of your internal territory until at least one of these achieves the esteemed role of "adopted value." That truth then becomes a supporting column holding up a new addition to your personality. You have grown, and you are now something more than you were before. Illness has expanded you, however painfully, fretfully, antagonistically, and even regretfully. Illness has become your master teacher!

Use This Book In Many Ways...

1. Read through it as you would any other book.

2. Use it as your daily meditation program. This is probably best accomplished by devoting an entire day to one of the 101 truths—reading through a particular reflection several times and keeping the first sentence in your mind throughout the day.

3. Use this book as a handy reference of insight—opening up to any page when the Spirit strikes you to search for spiritual sustenance.

4. Use it as a text for a class you might attend or you might decide to offer at your church, health care center, or another appropriate place.

5. Use this book as the beginning content for a support group for persons with illness and/or their caregivers.

Healing vs. Curing

Please take note that I use the word healing in this book and throughout the entire *Spiritual Strengths Inner Healing Series*. This is quite intentional in that I draw strict separation between healing on the one hand and curing on the other.

Curing refers to what the medical community hopes to offer you; it hopes to cure your sickness, your medical diagnosis. Healing is very different. Healing seeks to close the chasm that has opened up in you as a reaction to your sickness. My intention here is to help with your *illnesses* of your sickness—those personal, emotional, psychological, and/or spiritual reactions you experience as a result of your diagnosis. A short list of the illnesses of illness might include: anger, depression, anxiety, shame, guilt, irritability, hard heartedness, indifference, obtuseness, weakness, and insecurity just to name a few. All of these, and all the multiple human maladies that your shadows and compulsions bring on, are aspects of human suffering that the Spiritual Strengths Inner Healing Plan attempts to bring to God's healing.

The Spiritual Strengths Healing Profile

I make reference to "Spiritual Strengths" throughout this book. What are Spiritual Strengths? You are gifted with special strengths quite unique to your one-of-a-kind personality. The overall purpose or goal of your personality is to express the uniqueness of you. To accomplish this lifelong task, your personality is powered by grace (Spiritual Strengths). With this grace power, your personality is constantly performing six functions of which you are almost entirely unaware. These six are: 1) believing, 2) perceiving, 3) thinking, 4) feeling, 5) deciding, and 6) acting. Each one of these six personality functions is energized by a different Spiritual Strength. Each one of these strengths is quite intentionally given to you by God. Coincidentally, your six Spiritual Strengths together provide the necessary energy to heal your illnesses of illness.

You can discover your unique Spiritual Strengths by visiting: www.spiritualstrengthshealing.com. There you can take the Spiritual Strengths Healing Profile (SSHP), a 120-item scientifically valid and reliable questionnaire that will, in your 20-page personal report, pinpoint and describe not only your six "premier" Spiritual Strengths, but also bring you on a self-knowledge journey unlike any other, which will propel you to move you forward toward optimal healing.

> *A Final Note: I am a Christian by birth and practice, and I have no doubt that this lifetime faith walk shows through in these pages. Please don't infer from this bias that this book is only for Christians. I believe that the truths in these pages are universal. I've written them from a Christian perspective because it's the only one that is natural for me. If you are not a Christian, then I ask you to filter my bias so that my words ring clear and true to you. I thank you.*

Richard P. Johnson, Ph.D., CHC

101 Spiritual Truths that can Heal Your Illness

One

Illness teaches me that its true purpose is gaining closer communion with God.

The world sees no purpose in illness; illness is simply a malignant disease to be eradicated, poisoned, cutout, or otherwise disposed of as quickly as possible. Yet, might there be something more to illness, something of value?

If I were given the choice of living a life of ease, or living a life that ultimately brings me to my first source and center of life, the point from which all things flow...which would I choose?

Suppose my job in life is to gradually come closer and closer, and ultimately mesh into an intimate connection with God. Suppose that illness was one means, among many, to assist me in achieving this special communion? Would my illness still carry the same ominous weight of pathos that it does? Might I see my illness differently? Might I actually find value in it somewhere?

Can the tolls that my illness forces me to pay give me a new freedom, a new freedom to travel roads I would otherwise miss...roads that bring me to places of heart, and to people of soul, and to things of worth that I may have overlooked previously?

Today I grow closer to God.

Two

Illness teaches me that as my body diminishes, my spirit advances.

Strength of body and strength of soul may interact in an inverse way—as the one increases, the other decreases. When I scan illness's assault on my body from this perspective it invites me into a new vision, albeit a paradoxical one where my spiritual strengths are activated by the bodily losses I'm experiencing.

I can't wish healing for my illness as I might wish for a piece of chocolate, or some desired event or relationship. Illness plunges me into a sea that both frightens me and consoles me, both threatens me and cleanses me, and both strips me bare and clothes me in luxury.

Illness is a surprising teacher. On the one hand it takes so much away from me, but when I listen closer I can hear the call to patience. If I wait and allow the other hand to unfold, I find something I've wanted for so very long—a path of faith and hope that leads to a new balance and coherence of personality, new ways of opening-up my soul, and an illuminated mind, all of which can positively influence the course of my illness.

Today my spirit advances.

Three

Illness teaches me to live in a new abundance of inner light.

My illness has refocused my awareness on the divine light that pervades and innervates every bit of me, my body and blood, my strong parts and my weak (illness) parts. This light is the reflection of my spiritual strengths—the presence of the Spirit within me.

When I am in my spiritual strengths, then I am whole; my personality and my psyche operate optimally in the face of the illness invader. This light is a gift I can use or ignore as I choose.

Today I choose to center the divine inner light on those sites of illness in my body, where it envelops and heals them. I also focus the marvelous laser beam of God's light on my thoughts, gently asking the Spirit to soothe my fragmented thinking, ease any pain caused by my thoughts, and brighten any dark thoughts.

Today I am in new light.

Four

Illness teaches me to light the path to sacred healing.

My illness has pushed me onto a path that is not only steep and rugged, slippery and treacherous, but also scary and very, very dark. My spiritual strengths are strung as sacred lanterns along the path; torches of comfort and a testimony to God's prevailing power.

The lights of my spiritual strengths give surety to my footfalls and reassurance to my heart that while I must travel this path; I know that I'm not alone—ever!

Without these lights, I'm lost, abandoned, and afraid. Without these lights, hope is extinguished and replaced only by fear. I degenerate then into convulsions of fright that paralyze me and smother my spiritual strengths leaving me vulnerable to all of my shadows and compulsions. I become "not myself," my personality rebels and I use my mind in ways that do violence to me—I'm dark of mood and sad of affect; I demand and scold, I ridicule and criticize. All this is not me, but only the shadow of me frightened and in the dark.

Today I see light at the end of the tunnel of illness.

Five

Illness teaches me how to tend the garden of my soul.

My soul is a verdant garden where spiritual flowers bloom, fruits of faith ripen, and vegetables of a sacred type grow strong. But, among the sturdy, fresh, and supple shoots, I know my illness lurks as a poison, as a toxin, a killer that seeks to blindly destroy the abundance there.

My spiritual strengths are my tools and my reserve to root-out the illness weeds, to water the life back into the stems, to cut away the damaged parts, to add new fertilizer to a plant that's lost its luster, and to ensure sustaining life to this spot of ground that has always served me so well...and will again.

My spiritual strengths firmly root me in the ground. They provide light so I can grow, air that I can breathe, warmth to help me blossom, and water to quench my dryness and produce my fruit of the vine. My spiritual strengths connect my branches to the central vine of God's healing grace.

Today I devote all of my tending to my spiritual garden.

Six

Illness teaches me how to pursue personal and spiritual transformation.

My life is as it has always been, but it also is not. Changes unwanted and stark have visited me and have taken up residence in dark places of my body. What am I to do with such uninvited guests who refuse to leave—even at my insistence that they do?

I am called to the elegant solution—it is me that is called change! But this change cannot be some simplistic shift I temporarily hold only to return to my comfort when my illness threat is gone. No, I'm called to a much deeper change, indeed to a transformative change that renders me permanently and positively changed. My illness demands that I become different from what I was. My illness calls me to awaken to a new life, ever more conscious of my spiritual strengths and their power to make me new.

So much of me will be like it was, but in ways subtle and strong, partial and pervasive, barely detectible yet brawny, I will be different. As this mammoth life challenge of illness does eventually pass from me, I will be left with a legacy of constructive change that will not pass from me.

Today I pursue deep personal change.

Seven

Illness teaches me to embrace my True Self.

Illness asks so many questions; most I don't even know the answer to! But one question seems central: "Who am I?" Never before have I labored with such intensity to find the answer.

Just yesterday my life reflected a more simple response than today...I thought I knew who I was then. But yesterday's answers seem a bit hollow today; they seem not simple but simplistic in the face of my illness. I need a bigger and deeper answer. I can't be satisfied with small and shallow answers of yesterday anymore.

The self I thought I was appears today only as a shell of me, not the substance. I find myself groping for more. In some strange way, illness both reduces me and also enhances me greatly. My old self seems insufficient, but this newly emerging True Self is a robust, full-bodied expression of the fullness of my genuineness— the essence of and in my spiritual strengths.

Today I crave to be the realest me there is.

Eight

Illness teaches me to step beyond the "fake" of the world.

My illness has catapulted me into a new 'life space,' a new perspective. The "teaching" of the world, that I am a body and that my goal is bodily comfort, leaves me empty in the face of my illness, and makes me very uncomfortable.

Formerly I saw my body as the object of all pleasure; today I'm tempted (by my shadows and compulsions) to see my body as the source of all pain. I believe that neither is true and yet these antique thoughts persist and "fake" me into thinking that I can be taken away, that I can be separated from myself...yet deeper still in me I know the fallacy of this "fake."

I am the fullness of me; I am body, and mind, and spirit. I am all three together operating as a unit now—one cannot trump the others now. I am much more than body, much more than pleasure, much more than pain.

My spiritual strengths give clarity to this fact; they give me my true reality, my genuineness—stripped of any "fakes" the world may preach, denuded of any fraudulency pushed upon me by my shadows and compulsions.

Today I am sure in my spiritual strengths—I am not "fake." I am true!

Nine

Illness teaches me the paradox of living; that loss is my primary means for growth.

Illness takes things from me; sometimes I feel like I'm the victim of a continuously running robbery. Bit by bit, the thief of my illness takes from me what I possess.

Illness can take my livelihood, my monetary security, and even my home. It can take my friends (at least some who I thought were), my leisure, my strong body…it can even invade my self-esteem, my upbeat mood, my humor, my positive attitude, my intimacy, and more. But the real question is what impact do these losses have on the real me?

I'm called to respond to these losses differently. I need to mourn them fully, but beyond this I need to realize that what was lost is not insufferable. Even beyond this realization, I can understand that the losses do have power hidden inside them; they have implicit energy to move me to new growth.

Just as I was forced to give up my "toddlerhood" so many years ago so that I could grow into "childhood," I now give-up what illness takes from me physically so I can grow even more emotionally, psychologically, and most of all spiritually.

Today I know my losses do not define the real me.

Ten

Illness teaches me to become a spiritual self-healer through God's energy.

How do I best care for myself during this illness time? Certainly I learn to say a more definitive "yes" to my needs, and a more declarative "no" to what others, and I may only want.

I learn to feed my body and mind what they need to thrive during this dark time. I can nourish and strengthen my body, stimulate and challenge my mind; I can give rest when required, and a kick of motivation when necessary. All of this I can and do choose to do. Yet, beyond all this, how do I become a self-healer?

Healing is a gift from God that I so dearly desire. Healing (as distinct from curing) is promised to all, but to find healing God requires my full cooperation, my co-sponsorship. I self-heal only in partnership with the Spirit who continually offers me the power and might of the energy/grace resident in those spiritual strengths that the Holy One has bequeathed to me. My gifted spiritual strengths are my special healing tools.

Today I fly to my spiritual strengths as my healing salvation.

Eleven

Illness teaches me to become more comfortably "who" I am.

Again I find the question of my true "who" arises. Illness may strip me of my "what," the ways the world identifies and defines me: my profession, my "status," my lifestyle, my ownership, and the like. Illness is a skillful surgeon that slices away the unnecessary of me and cuts to the core of who I am. Illness can take all of this, but illness cannot take my core.

There, at the core, I find not bone and sinew, not blood and bile, but the essence of God's love awaiting my discovery and my call. This grace is truly me, these gifts, my spiritual strengths, are the presence of the Spirit, not separate or distinct from me, as something foreign, but the actual core of me, the center point and place of me, not the setting but the spiritual substance of me.

The "who" of me is more than that which gives me character, it is beyond form and function, it is power, energy, might, and intelligence...it is the God-presence "Who" of me that pulsates healing at my epicenter.

Today I am closer to the "who" God says I am.

Twelve

Illness teaches me to seek love everywhere.

Before my illness I was overly restrictive where I looked for love, consequently I found love only in particular and selected places and people. It wasn't that I was looking for love in "wrong" places, only too few places.

Love of course comes only from God; indeed we define God as Love, and Love as God. Illness has taught me to vastly broaden my perspective of Love; I now look for love where God resides; and because God resides everywhere, I look for love there and only there—everywhere!

I'm certainly not always successful in my search for love; I'm still working hard to see love in my illness. But, little by little, I'm scrapping together a new vision of love and loving that is motivated by my perceiving spiritual strength. This new vision of love sees beyond the physically obvious all the way to the mystery of God's intentions.

Rather than the plain truth, illness has taught me to look for God's mysterious truth. I know I can never understand God's mystery, but I can try, and in the trying I'm training my vision and getting closer each day. Lord, help me to live more by faith and less by sight.

Today I seek Love everywhere.

Thirteen

Illness teaches me to honor close relationships.

My illness has a way of opening the portals of my awareness to my truest realities, and simultaneously diminishing those I formerly mistook as real. My former blindedness extended to how I valued relationships. Across the spectrum of relationship from closest to most distant, I can now see that I viewed others through the crude and self-centered shade of utility...what can this relationship do for me?

My assumption was that all relationships were supposed to somehow serve me—if there was no way of getting something from the relationship, then there was no reason to be in it. I didn't consciously realize this before my illness, but illness has sharpened me to know it now.

Now I respect the individual and the relationship with an honor that extends to the sacred. My question is no longer, *"How can this person serve me?"* Rather my question is, *"How can I serve this person?"* My illness has taught me that the only way I can serve others is to first see the divinity in them.

Today I honor all my relationships.

$\mathcal{F}ourteen$

Illness teaches me to live the holy present moment...now

I was angry when I was first diagnosed with illness. I assumed that my illness would shorten my life, that it would take time away from me. I didn't realize that I worshipped the god of longevity. I thought that the longer I lived; the more birthdays I celebrated, the better for me.

Once I could drop this veil of anger, I could better see that I lived in the future—today was only valuable for what it brought for tomorrow. Illness has shown me the value of today quite apart from the future. I'm not promised a future. I'm only given today; indeed, I'm only given "now." This "now" is only valuable to the degree that I choose to make it valuable.

My illness teaches me that the "now" is much more than a measure of time; it is a heartbeat of the eternal, which makes the "now" a sacred instant. The "now" can be an inspirational moment to the degree that I invest it with the vitality of my spiritual strengths. When I connect this "now" with the eternal presence of God in me, whatever the moment is, I realize just how packed with the power of the Almighty this "now" is for me.

Today I live in the holy present...the "now."

Fifteen

Illness teaches me that my "illness time" can be my finest spiritual hour.

Before my current illness time, I was so driven by productivity, by producing "things," to the degree that I only saw "my finest hours" as those times of greatest personal production. Any year that passed without generating a new book was at least uninspiring if not wasteful to me.

I still "produce" books, but I no longer need to for *my* self. My finest hours are now those spent with God in the presence of my spiritual strengths.

When a final accounting of my life is taken, what moments will stand out as my finest hours? My illness has given me a new answer to this question. My time with illness with its struggles, its doubts, fears, pain, and expense...all of its demands will, I believe, be counted as at least one of my finest hours indeed.

Today I live as this is my finest hour.

Sixteen

Illness teaches me the power and necessity of forgiveness.

Before my illness I saw forgiveness in its most elementary form. I saw it as a simple "I-thou" endeavor. Either "I" let "thou" off the hook for something you did "wrong" to me, or "thou" did the same for me. Forgiveness was a simple accounting item; I could forgive you if you would forgive me, and vice versa. In my old ways of thinking I forgave because I wanted something in return, even if that something was only calming my conscience.

My illness has brought forgiveness to new and deeper levels for me. Forgiveness has become a way of life for me now. I'm a long way from achieving this, and perhaps I never will, but I now see forgiveness as blessing, and I imagine that everything and everyone in this world needs my blessing—my forgiveness, and I need their blessing. Naturally this includes illness; it too needs my forgiveness—my blessing. When I bless with forgiveness, I stop fighting.

I'm now accepting illness, not with any resignation or submission, but with new and true spiritual grit of reality that inspires my spiritual healing strengths to new levels of effectiveness.

Today I forgive my illness.

Seventeen

Illness teaches me that I have no more need for anger.

Anger is the emotional reaction I experience when I criticize another, when I judge them or their behavior as "wrong." Certainly there are lots of "bad" behaviors out there, but illness has taught me to look for what's right and to try to overlook what's wrong or "bad."

Being wrong or doing badly isn't noteworthy in my new time of illness. What is noteworthy is what's good, what's virtuous, what's from the Spirit. It's these things I try hard to focus upon. As I progress in my illness-induced journey and I work hard at getting out of the "judgment business," I find less and less need for anger. I'm out of the criticism business; the world doesn't need another critic.

My illness has taught me that the world needs lovers not judgers. My new job, especially now with illness as my companion, is to be a lover. Illness asks me to live in love more than fear, in love more than criticism, in love more than trying to control things so they come out "right," i.e., the way I want them to turn out.

Today I put anger aside.

Eighteen

Illness teaches me the immense value of "letting go."

Illness has induced me to ask whether I am holding onto any expectations, assumptions, presumptions, or thoughts that may have now become a restraint, encumbrance, or block to my forward healing progression. Put another way, what am I refusing to let go of that I need to?

Sometimes I see myself as Tarzan swinging through the jungle (illness can seem like a deep, dark and foreboding jungle) from vine to vine. What would happen if Tarzan didn't let go of a vine? Eventually he would be left hanging from that vine going nowhere. I felt like that when I was diagnosed, I was hanging in the jungle and had no place to go, no forward movement.

My spiritual strengths forced me to look at how I was using my personality. What beliefs and attitudes needed to be dumped? What point of view needed recycling? What thoughts needed vitalizing? What feelings were holding my healing captive? What decisions had I made that were now acting as quicksand? And what new actions were necessary now.

Today I choose to let go of all that blocks my healing.

Nineteen

Illness teaches me that I feel best when I give of myself.

My illness is a hard teacher; it has a way of showing me just how stupid I've been, just how selfish I've allowed my life to become.

Left unchecked by adversity, we all remain "takers." Illness reminds me that my true calling is that of "giver." Giving bears many benefits. I simply feel better when I help someone, I feel a warm heart, fewer aches and pains, less depressed, stronger, and have more energy.

My shadows and compulsions beckon me to seek things from others, even if it's only their pity, as a means of raising my importance, or giving me a new role to play. All this ultimately brings only disappointment and dependency.

My spiritual strengths tell me the opposite: *Give away what you have*, they say. Give away *your* self and show interest in another, give away your smile, your kind words, your compassionate look, your affirming blessing—give away yourself and feel better.

Today I give myself to others.

Twenty

Illness teaches me to find a new freshness in living by celebrating my faith.

I've always practiced my faith; I've always gone through the motions that my faith prescribes. But it is my illness that teaches me how to celebrate the fact that I am truly loved by God, that I am unique among all, and that I am beloved and even cherished.

Illness introduces me to a self I didn't know that I had. Illness lets me know myself better, helps me see my faith as the treasure it is, propels me to value its inherent power for healing, and its capacity for making me brand new. Illness deepens me and makes me more reverent of all that is. My Illness lets me see my faith through new eyes, and compels me to listen with new ears to the words of worship, and learn to appreciate their simple yet profound beauty.

My illness pushes me to become more obedient to my faith, not because I am trying to "get my house in order," but just because my new reverence shows me it's clearly the right thing to do. My illness pushes me to my knees, sometimes in gratitude and other times in pain, because at times there is nowhere else to go, and there is nothing else I can do, but fall to my knees in prayer.

Today I celebrate.

Twenty-one

Illness teaches me the true purpose of life...to become "living virtue."

One of the kindest gifts my illness has given me is a new life direction, or rather a new reason for a life direction that I've previously tried to pursue.

I've always known (and tried to follow) my life purpose as a helper to others. While I've tried to be faithful to this purpose, I was blind to a good portion of my real motivation behind it. I now see that a portion of my motivation was to benefit myself. Oh, I was as altruistic as I could be in my blinded state, but nonetheless, I was generally self-interested and self-directed. My illness has changed this; illness has put me on a new course to be more God-directed.

My new revelation is not simply to practice virtue, but incredibly to <u>be</u> virtue. I certainly have been a hopeful person over the years, but now I seek not simply to practice hope but to be hope. I strove to be kind, now I strive to be kindness. I sought to be compassionate, but now I see my calling as compassion itself. I know that I can never be hope, or kindness, or compassion completely, but in holding this goal in mind, I find new purpose and new motivation. Illness has elevated me, even caused me to see the exalted place God offers me.

Today I am virtue!

Twenty-two

Illness teaches me the ultimate failure of life is not death; the ultimate failure of life is living without love.

Dying has always been my most terrifying personal fear. Survival was the goal at all costs. I poured my physical and mental energies into a search for security, a quest to stay alive and stay as comfortable being alive as possible. This is certainly a noble goal, but it is one that becomes gradually tempered by the reality of death somewhere "out there" on the remote horizon.

My illness has changed this; death is a more proximate probability now. My illness has allowed me to make friends with death. I know now that God loves me still whether I'm alive on this plane, or not. While I'm in the state of material aliveness, what matters most now is not primarily the avoidance of death (although I certainly do all I can to stay alive) but what I do, or how I practice being in love.

What a gift this is, what a grand relief to know this new purpose! Yet it foists a new responsibility on me, a responsibility for placing myself in the flow of love, so that I can be a promoter not an inhibitor of love. My new love purpose invites me to pray, and pray, and pray.

Today I am healed.

Twenty-three

Illness teaches me that my feelings are holy, in that they give me insight into where I need to change.

For years, indeed my whole pre-illness life, I think I fought my feelings. I either fought paralyzing, negative feelings away, or fought to attract enhancing, enriching and positive feelings to me. My life with my feelings was a constant fight.

My illness caused me to shift from this bellicose stance and adopt a new posture toward feelings. Now I see my feelings as invitations for change. Certainly this is true for my more noxious feelings.

When I feel an emotion that I'd rather not have, I simply ask the feeling, through the power of my feeling function spiritual strength, what change it is asking of me. Invariably the change it signals is one in the way I use my personality—the way I choose to use the spiritual strengths I've been given.

Today I find new insight into my feelings.

Twenty-four

Illness teaches me to live life balanced in the Spirit.

Balance comes in two varieties, internal and external.

External balance refers to the ways I allot my physical and mental energies among the various arenas of my life: work, family, relationships, self, leisure, and spirit. I am balanced when I devote relatively equal measures of life energy among these six.

Internal balance refers to how close to the center point of my spiritual strengths I am, and away from the extreme positions of my shadows and compulsions.

My illness gives me new impetus to look at my life with a more sensitive touch and a clearer vision, so I can adjust both my internal and external balance points with new accuracy. When I seek new balance using my spiritual strengths, healing quite naturally follows...it's almost effortless. I don't need to strain, or push, or ever-exert myself to experience healing now; I simply need to rest gently in my spiritual strengths, and almost automatically I take another step along my healing path.

Today I seek balance to move closer to healing.

Twenty-five

Illness teaches me that my spiritual pace quickens as I mature in my response to illness.

My illness journey draws me deeper and deeper into my interior, and as I go, and especially as I can let go of all that is unnecessary in my life, I find new freedom, and a great unburdening of my spirit. All this gives rise to a gradual uptick in the pace of my spiritual growth.

My spiritual dynamics begin to spin more rapidly, and as they do, they generate ever more spiritual energy that is now readily available for healing. This process requires that I move beyond reacting to my illness and begin responding to it.

Reactions are "fighting against," automatic reflexes that originate in the more reflexive autonomic mechanism of my being. Responses are "learning from" actions of intention that originate in the deeper core of my advancing spiritual personality.

Today I respond and find my spiritual pace quickening.

Twenty-six

Illness teaches me to distinguish between the "what" of me, and the "who" of me.

My illness pushes the "what" of me aside. My illness doesn't care about my profession, it has no interest in my financial status, it is indifferent to my social standing, and it has never even heard of athletic, travel, philanthropic, or other personal accomplishments and/or experiences. My illness is quite blind to the "what" of me.

On the other hand, my illness seems vitally interested in the "Who" of me. Illness shifts my focus away from what my personality produces, and toward how I use it. I now realize that the "Who" of me is best portrayed by the level and degree to which I can call upon and manifest my six premier spiritual strengths in my life.

Productivity is irrelevant, what matters is reflecting the energy of my strengths onto how I use my personality. How closely do my beliefs reflect my believing strength? Do my views reflect my perceiving strength? Are my thoughts aligned with my thinking strength? Are my emotions in sync with my feeling strength?

Today I seek to show my true "Who" through my strengths.

Twenty-seven

Illness teaches me to reframe my view of illness from a "world view" to a "soul-view."

In my former life before illness, I thoughtlessly adopted the current cultural view of illness—a morbid and simplistic view that mistakenly equated illness with diminishment and even death. I inadvertently avoided persons who were ill because I consciously didn't know what to say to them, and because I unconsciously was afraid that I'd catch their illness from them.

Once the initial toxic emotions abated after the tumult of my illness diagnosis, I began to change my view of illness and I took on a more philosophical or spiritual perspective.

I noticed that something more happened as I gradually turned my personality toward my spiritual strengths, and especially as my perceiving strength advanced, I noticed a distinct shift toward what I'd call a soul-view of illness, a view that didn't see illness as a medical diagnosis at all, but saw it as a condition of my soul.

Today I reframe my view of illness.

Twenty-eight

Illness teaches me to rely on that small but potent inner voice of the Spirit for guidance in my everyday decision making.

My illness has sharpened my hearing, at least my internal hearing. Only recently have I given much thought to what or whom I was listening to for guidance and direction. Now I'm keenly aware of the "voices" in me and where they originate.

I have more than several voices that speak to me (not actual voices, but spiritual ones), some are premier strengths voices, others are shadow voices, and the rest are compulsion voices. I'm becoming more adept at discerning which voices are speaking to me at any given time, what they are saying, and how best to respond.

The spiritual strengths voices are soft and tender, but can be easily drown out by shadow voices which are pleading, sometimes a bit squeaky, and certainly different from compulsion voices that are authoritative, demanding, and even haughty sounding. Differentiating among these becomes easier with practice. The small voice, the faint breath felt gently is the most important one now, the others are in contrast and much more strident and shrill.

Today I listen to my small inner voice.

Twenty-nine

Illness teaches me that wellness is as much a spiritual concept as it is physical and mental.

Wellness is a holistic concept that includes being healthy of body, wise of mind, and whole of spirit. I was quite familiar with the first two before my illness, but the third wellness competency that dealt with the spiritual realm presented me a challenge. I never gave spiritual wellness much thought before, but I do now that I realize its deep impact upon my healing.

Spiritual wellness includes injecting integrity, or cohesiveness, into my personality; having a sense of inner potency that gives me confidence to act; seeing all the events of my life through the lens of God; and making my connection with God the central guiding principle of my life now. I can honestly say that the losses of illness have been my spiritual coaches for all of this new learning.

Spiritual wellness is devoting each and every day to a different one of my spiritual strengths and trying to live in this strength all day long. All this gives a wonderful message of unity and a dramatically clearer recognition of the genuine priorities of life now that I'm traveling with my illness.

Today is my time for new spiritual wellness.

Thirty

Illness teaches me that my true wealth is not measured with a calculator.

Before my illness, and without consciously realizing it, I was determining my wealth and my personal worth based on my monetary and property resources. We're all so steeped in such thinking as primary imprints in a capitalistic culture that we hardly give our views on the sources of wealth a second thought.

But again, my illness provided the impetus for me to re-evaluate just where my true wealth resides. It became obvious that my wealth squarely resides in my spiritual strengths. Wealth is what gives security for well-being; it's that which provides longevity of value.

My former interest in accumulating monetary wealth has now shifted to accumulating spiritual wealth by doing what I can to strengthen the impact my spiritual strengths have on the functioning of my personality. I try to practice adept spiritual wealth management techniques for longitudinal wealth preservation—fully aware that all spiritual strengths are gifts from God, I cannot create them or even hold them; I can, however, position myself to take full advantage of them.

Today I measure my wealth with the yardstick of my spiritual strengths.

Thirty-one

Illness teaches me that that peace is internal, not external.

Before my illness, whenever we prayed for peace at church I always brought up mental images of world peace or restoring peace in a war-torn area or country. For me, the notion of peace was clearly external.

Now when we pray for peace, in my post-illness diagnosis stage, vastly different images pop up in my mind's eye. I now see peace as an "inside job" that begins with God, is captured by and compacted into my spiritual strengths, and is reflected out from me.

I see my spiritual strengths soothing my heart, mind, and soul; and I extend that grace of peace to everyone in the sanctuary, and then to everyone in our community, region, state, province, country. Finally I envision the reign of peace enveloping the hearts and minds of people throughout the entire world. Truly I feel the peace of God in my heart even though the world (or parts of it) is in chaos.

Today I find peace in my heart.

Thirty-two

Illness teaches me that I must always have dreams.

Everything changed for me on the day when my doctor said, *"I'm sorry, but you have an illness!"* At that moment I was pushed into an entirely new way of using all six functions of my personality. Strangely, I noticed that over time my thoughts actually became clearer, especially thoughts about the future. From the depths of me emerged the question, *"And now what?"*

I guess my experience isn't unique but rather common—evidence the movie *The Bucket List* (directed by Rob Reiner, 2007, written by Justin Zackhau, Warner Bros.). What did I want to <u>do</u> that I hadn't yet? But then the question morphed into, *"How do I want to <u>be</u> now?"* It was an exhilarating question that brought me to the center of my soul, right to the gifts that God had entrusted to me.

I realized that God made me to love, actually to <u>be</u> love. So my new dream needed to be something about learning how to love better now that I had my illness. This became my new quest, to marshal all the love-energy in my spiritual strengths and become a diamond of love reflecting the true reality of me to whomever God brought to me now. And I soon realized that my illness journey brought lots of new people to me in brand new ways.

Today my dream quest captivates my soul.

Thirty-three

Illness teaches that I function best when I have a personal cause, passion, goal, or purpose that is bigger than me.

I discovered that "being in love" anew is a noble, even celestial motivation. But being human, and living on the material plane as I do, I longed for something practical, something specific, and something absolutely congruent with my over-arching purpose of love that I could embrace as "my project," my goal, and my unique objective.

I think writing this book about what I've learned from illness is part of that goal, a goal that flows from the vision of Love in me. Thankfully I can bring this overall goal into material reality by writing, speaking, teaching, counseling, providing spiritual direction, and so forth. With love as my overall purpose, my goal necessarily needs to revolve around helping God's people see their truth, beauty, and goodness.

I'm given a purpose by helping others, and once that purpose is firmly in place in my personality, I'm further gifted with all the fantastic spiritual strengths that are required to bring this God-purpose into reality. I seek closer relationship with God by being in relationship with God's people.

Today I live my life on purpose.

Thirty-four

*Illness teaches me to have fun:
activities that rejuvenate my body,
stimulate my mind, and/or enrich my
soul.*

When I was first diagnosed with my illness, I threw myself into the "land of illness" by reading, learning, questioning, investigating, etc., etc., etc., about illness.   Ultimately I found myself consumed in and by my illness. Illness had not only invaded my body, but it had also overtaken my mind. I needed a break.

I then discovered the psychology of leisure and its primary and paradoxical tenet, "I must regularly vacate my routines in order to remain focused upon them."   My routines now all revolved around my illness, so it was illness that I needed to "regularly vacate." But how could I achieve this...and by what means? I needed to have fun.

Fun removes me from my routines; it gives me a vacation from illness. I struggle with this because, while I enjoy fun and vacations, I've always been a bit guilty about them because...well...I can't get anything done!

I started working on leisure, but quickly realized the contradiction here. I now try to "flow" with the moment by finding my leisure, my fun, contemplation, discussion, social interaction, and spectator appreciation (I like to watch people).

Today I find fun.

Thirty-five

Illness teaches me to see my illness as a call for change.

Change is the watchword of the universe; there is not one thing in the universe that is not in constant change...only God doesn't change. I am a member of this universe and so I am charged with change as well.

Change occurs in me whether I'm aware of it or not. On the physical level, this unconscious change is quite functional. I don't need to be aware of the operation of my GI tract to digest my breakfast food. But, on the mental and spiritual levels change requires my conscious awareness. Without my active intention, change is generally not additive, constructive, and/or positive for me; on these levels I need to be fully awake to change.

I need to exercise my own volition, to make free will choices about the change I want and need. The more awake I am, the better the change for me. Illness has awakened me; it has captured my attention and made me very, very open to change.

Today I live in change.

Thirty-six

Illness teaches me to see beauty, seek delight, and be in awe always.

The more awake I become, the more I realize that I live in a beautiful and fruitful garden. I am part of this garden…I am fruitful as well. Indeed, I am one with this beautiful garden—I am fruit and fruitful, I am (and so are you) the ripening produce of God's hand.

My illness has given me this insight that brings a triumphant solace to my heart knowing that I am part of the circle of life that God has created. Illness doesn't remove me from the garden; illness has mysteriously planted me there more firmly in the deep hummus of grace. In this place I find awe and delight; I am without words to describe its beauty.

In medical terms, I guess I could say that I'm now taking a new drug…the drug of grace. In spiritual terms, I see that illness has lifted me up to a higher place where I can see the same terrain I always have but with vastly keener eyes; I see a new terrain that is clearer, wider, broader, and more inwardly potent than I've ever seen before.

Today I live in beauty, delight, and awe.

Thirty-seven

Illness teaches me to give my burdens to God.

My illness has burdened me with cares I never experienced before. Some cares are material, some are emotional, some mental, and others spiritual. Each of these burdens clamors for resolution. I seek harmony and I find myself in chaos. What do I do?

When I seek solutions on the material plane I find frustration, incomplete answers, and only fragmented and unreliable tools to restore what the illness has taken from me. I need to look in another place to find relief for my burdens. This other place is not "out there" but "in here."

My illness has taught me to look inside for the answers my heart seeks. There I find the altar of God where I place all my cares, my turmoil, my burdens, my fears, and all that troubles me. I bow before the altar and gently place all my burdens in front of the Almighty. I can exit my little internal chapel with new feelings of release. I am now unburdened for I know that which truly burdens me I made myself.

Today I am unburdened.

Thirty-eight

Illness teaches me the value of a "confidante" relationship.

I know that St. Francis claimed that it is better to understand than to be understood, but, oh, how I long to be understood; how I strive in so many ways to hear from another human being their sweet understanding of exactly "where I am" in my journey with illness.

I seek the solace of a forgiving and compassionate companion who seems to know what I'm saying and feeling, even without me fully expressing it. Another human, so "tuned-in" and so connected with the emotions of my struggle that at points we almost merge into a unity of graceful recognition that we are both souls on a trek, each with our separate living to do, but each strangely connected in the spiritual strength of empathy—soul knowing.

This spiritual confidante seems to see me clearer and know my emotions even better than I see and know them myself. Oh, what a gift this confidante is! Oh, what a joy! And to think that it was illness that allowed this to happen. Oh happy turmoil!

Today I see the gift of a confidante, a companion on my journey.

Thirty-nine

Illness teaches me that my illness time can be one of emotional and spiritual vitality and vibrancy.

To live vitally means to inject the present moment with its full measure of life and love; it means searching for the Spirit-spark that exists right here, right now; it means being proactive, positive, and spontaneous without being impulsive; it means living to the fullest extent possible even under whatever conditions illness may be thrusting in my face.

Vitality means resiliently developing a mental attitude that lets me face facts, but doesn't let even the harshest facts wash me out to sea.

Vitality means never letting the light of the Spirit within me go out; never separating myself from the vibrant flow of energy-grace that the Spirit continuously showers upon me.

Vitality is my gift, and my illness can enhance it, or, if I let it, my illness can do the opposite.

Today I live in spiritual vitality and vibrancy.

Forty

Illness teaches me how to better care for myself.

My illness can sometimes drain my spiritual energies; my illness can wear me out. The medications that may be injected into me and other treatments that penetrate into me all take their toll on my health, my stamina, and my perseverance.

My illness is a paradox, at one and the same time illness can build me up spiritually, while it tears me down emotionally and physically. As illness has taught me to give my burdens over to God, likewise illness teaches me to shift my attitudes about caring.

In my pre-illness years, I thought it better to give care than to receive it. Now my needs are different; they call me to modify my care-giving and care-receiving attitudes. In the grand economy of God's love, at different times in my life, I'm sometimes called at to give more, while at others to receive more. In my illness time I have dropped whatever needs I had to always "play" the giver because now is a time when I'm called to receive more than give.

Yet, I'm not supposed to be a passive receiver; rather I'm to be an active one by being clear about my needs and by asking directly for help. I can't assume that others will know my needs, so I must be intentional about my requests and grateful in my acceptance of care.

Today I care for myself.

Forty-one

Illness teaches me to be kinder and more generous to my body.

As I become freer in asking others for their assistance, I must also be freer to give myself the help that only I can give to myself. My body groans for support, and at times I grumble (or worse) trying to find the spot that needs some soothing touch (sometimes I don't even know what that is) that I long to receive.

How can I be generous to my own needs; how can I best be kind to myself in the midst of the terror raging in those dark broken places in my body? I must practice a tough kindness by prodding, cajoling, arguing, and then pushing myself to be generous and kind to my body.

And how do I care for myself? I need to eat well; I need to exercise regularly; I need to moderate my stress; I need to rest; and I need to allow a tender touch.

I also care for myself by resolving old conflicts, by giving and receiving love, by appreciating humor, by making considered choices, by sustaining myself through suffering, and by squarely facing what I may have formerly denied myself. Such is the tough-love kind of curriculum of self-generosity that I'm called to by my faith in God and my respect for my well-being.

Today I am generous to my body.

Forty-two

Illness teaches me to master the psychology of leisure.

Leisure is a fundamental human need—a requirement of my soul. When I have no leisure, I risk a general erosion of my spirit; my spiritual strengths begin to wane and my shadows and compulsions gradually wax. Leisure can fill the empty places in me when I've spent all other personal resources.

All leisure is not created equal—my preferred leisure may be another's tedium. Illness has underscored for me that I do indeed need leisure, and during my illness time I need it all the more.

Leisure comes in many flavors: social interaction, spectator appreciation, creative expression, intellectual stimulation, physical exercise, and solitary relaxation—all is leisure. Leisure relieves the built-up stress that's accumulates in the fibers of my mind, body, and soul. It unwinds my muscles and my brain when I'm knotted up. It offers me respite and refreshment in the harsh, demanding, and arid terrain of illness.

Leisure gives me pause to be something other than a patient, so I can remind myself of who I really am before anything else. Leisure diverts me from the morbidity of illness and rejuvenates my soul. Oh, how sweet! Thank you, Lord.

Today I lose myself in leisure.

Forty-three

Illness teaches me to take charge of my life in new ways.

I sometimes wonder aloud how I managed my life before my illness. What were the principles upon which I based my life? What values were most prominent for me? It seems to me now that I was adrift then.

But now I feel like I've learned how to take the reins of my life in new ways. I have a new healthy assertiveness that allows me to be intensely engaged in a vital participation with all those assisting my journey, and especially with God. I'm now able to set life priorities that enable me to be much more intentional about how I see things, the way I think and feel about them, the decisions I make, and the actions that I take.

I've learned to live in a more relaxed fashion—dropping expectations and "going with the flow of life" rather than against it. Finally, illness has taught me an entirely new attitude about discomfort. Before my illness, I was intolerant of discomfort. Now I see discomfort as my teacher. Oh, I don't like discomfort, I certainly try to avoid it, but I'm not afraid of it anymore. This shift alone has allowed a new freedom I can't even describe.

Today I take new charge of my life.

Forty-four

Illness teaches me to be involved in a personal and continuous self-improvement program.

How can I be as well as possible even with my illness? How can I stretch to optimal health and well-being even as I'm assailed by illness? In the past I would have scoffed at such questions; now I know how relevant they are for stepping out of the victim role that I sometimes fall into.

My illness does not exempt me from striving to live fully; rather it invites me to ever-higher levels of self-health care motivation. My goal today is to thrive, not merely survive—stretching toward health improvement, not just health maintenance. I cannot change my illness, but there is much about my overall health that I can change.

The key to this change I've learned is in how I open my unique personality to the healing power within me—my healing spiritual strengths. My strengths always give me the option of improving my overall well-being. I can change my thoughts; I can change my feelings; I do have choices; I can smile; and I can act differently. I now realize that change is necessary for me, not as an option but as a requirement. What is the most health-enhancing behavior I can perform right now?

Today I resolve to improve my overall health.

Forty-five

Illness teaches me to rely on my internal wisdom that is powered by the Holy Spirit.

Illness helps me learn a new art of living wisely. The wisdom inherent in my spiritual strengths bestows insight, good sense, sound judgment, and the ability to discern inner qualities that I didn't know I had.

Wisdom illuminates my mind and lightens my heart. Wisdom vitalizes my thinking so I can take full responsibility for shifting my thoughts to a fuller mental wellness of clarity, soundness, and quality. My spiritual strengths give me power, a new intangible confidence in how I see myself, which offers the prospect of an exciting new role of living. I now see myself as sufficiently resourceful and capable of tackling what I need to so I can live in the abundance of wisdom.

Knowing my spiritual strengths empowers me, but this sacred illumination also gives me the added benefit of knowing my weaknesses. Illness squeezes me to such a degree that it threatens to drain me dry. When I know my points of vulnerability I quite naturally develop the means to convert the threat of illness into a challenge of illness.

Today I can meet the challenge of illness with wisdom.

Forty-six

Illness teaches me to express myself intimately...from my heart, and spiritually...from my soul.

Illness has opened my eyes to the immense value of relationships. I now cherish all my relationships, even some that formerly challenged my patience. It is only in a relationship that I can express/share what is most dear, important, relevant, and/or self-expressive to me.

Sharing the deepest parts of me, even my secrets, fears, guilt, failures, as well as my joys, delights, triumphs, and accomplishments, is not just important...it's vital for my health, happiness, and healing. I truly need to express myself, otherwise I begin to psychologically and spiritually wither—eventually I literally lose my will to live. Without a strong will to live, any and all illness treatment is weakened.

When I can express the core of me, I'm tapping into a reservoir of healing energy that is freeing, refreshing, and even exhilarating; I not only simply feel better, I actually <u>am</u> better. Before my illness I was somewhat indifferent about expressing my inner self for many reasons, but mostly because I didn't see the point of it. I didn't see that anything would change.

Today I express myself fully.

Forty-seven

Illness teaches me to learn the wise art of exceptional living—embracing change.

Living well with illness is always a story of integrating change into my personality. Illness pushes and prods me, it cramps and chaffs me, and it can even torture and torment me. I'm not called to resist all this as much as I am called to rearrange how I've been using the six functions of my personality.

Change means finding new ways of reallocating my life energy in ways that allow me a life of deeper meaning and heightened purpose. If I want to be happy while I'm in my illness journey (and not all persons with illness do), I can't dig in my heels and refuse the reality of my illness; rather I'm called to open up to change in ways I've never thought of before. I can't hold on to believing, perceiving, thinking, feeling, deciding, and acting in ways that worked for me yesterday but only hold me back today.

I need to listen to the voices of my spiritual strengths—ever-beckoning me to shift away from what were yesterday's facts but are now only unusable fantasies—to a new set of realizations and actions that become today's accurate and motivational strategies.

Today I practice exceptional living.

Forty-eight

Illness teaches me to practice a positive mental attitude (PMA).

It is me, and no one else, who is in charge of my mood. If and when I'm irritable, it's because I'm not using my personality optimally. Even though my inclination is to blame others or may illness for my foul mood, I know the root of my angst is in me.

Illness teaches me that my attitude needs changing. I need and want a more positive mental attitude, I want to remain mentally fit, attitudinally tough when needed, alert to beliefs and perceptions that can drag me down, and vigilant to culling out thoughts that can harm me.

To keep my energy up, I need to fix my mind on the source of all energy—God's presence within me in the form of my spiritual strengths. When I feed my mind a steady diet of negativism, not only does my mind and mood collapse, but also my body reacts by moving toward depression.

Illness teaches me how to move beyond the mental ruts that formerly plagued me by always consulting my spiritual strengths. They are the straightest roads to a positive mental attitude and peak performance.

Today I embody a PMA.

Forty-nine

Illness teaches me to move toward personal integration.

I strive to be integrated, having all parts of my personality operating "in sync." Personality integration leads to the spiritual condition of wholeness.

The aspect of wholeness that I now find most comforting for me is seeing what's happening to me as God might see it, and beginning to tiptoe into a fuller unity with God. As this process unfolds, all my personality functions start aligning with God as they orbit in a synchronous flow around the reinvigorating center point of my life.

One signal that informs me I'm approaching integration is the thought that there's *"more of me yet to become."* Even with my illness, and perhaps because of it, I know I'm still growing; I'm still evolving into something more than I was yesterday. This is a most soothing thought; it reassures me that there is purpose to my life even when I can't see it. I am alive, I am a reality, I am "me," and it is "me" who is with God, perhaps even more now that I'm traveling in the land of illness.

Today I imagine myself perfectly integrated.

Fifty

Illness teaches me to move from success to significance.

When I possess a sense of meaning it gives me the consoling thought that my life is somehow "on target," that I am living a life that is good, and true, and even beautiful. Having meaning gives me that profound pleasure that I am part of something bigger than me, something grand and wonderful.

Before my illness, I thought of my life as either a success or a failure. Now I think in terms of what degree my life is significant instead of successful. Significance is different from success. Success is measured essentially as an external, while significance is internal. Someone else determines my success, while it's only me that can experience and confer significance.

What had significance for me before my illness has changed now. Before my illness something was significant only to the degree it furthered my success. Now significance comes from feeling I'm a part of God's larger plan. My response to my illness, indeed all my responses to illness is what confers success and significance now. When I'm "in love," i.e., in my spiritual strengths, then I am living a significant life.

Today I live in significance.

Fifty-one

Illness teaches me to energize my creativity through grace.

Living with illness demands new creativity. In the past, before my illness, most of my creativity was expressed in writing. I still write, but now with illness as my companion, I see creativity best expressed in learning new ways of living.

It takes, I believe, immense creativity to develop a healthy dependence on God. To discover God in the deepest part of me takes a new creativity, a disciplined, quiet, unannounced creativity that is only motivated by grace. I'm much more aware of the movement of grace now. I'm sure grace always operated in me, but now my illness raises a heightened spiritual sensitivity in me that teaches me just how special I am, and that this specialness comes from being connected to God through grace.

Grace is the healing power and might of God. Grace pervades and innervates me, it's in me, around me, beside me, and under me…it's everywhere. Creativity is coming to recognize what grace is and realize that grace is my only true power.

Today, God's grace animates my creativity.

Fifty-two

Illness teaches me to "own" my whole, authentic self.

Life is a personal trek toward deeper discovery of my own personal authenticity. The trek includes all the twists and turns of life. Right now illness is part of my life; it has captured my attention.

I have a choice here. I have the choice of how I will relate to my illness with all that it takes from me and brings to me. Beyond this I also have a choice of which part of me I allow to take the primary lead personality position in that relating process...my world self, or my authentic self.

The degree to which I give my world self the lead is the same degree to which I will seek to rely on things of the world for my survival. Likewise, the degree to which I give my authentic self (my Holy self, my God self...the unique self of my soul) the lead position is the same degree to which I rely on the power of the ultimate divinity of God for my survival.

In the quiet of my soul I find the solace and direction to persevere, and in my spiritual strengths I find the power and confidence I need to capture and use the grace God gives me. I see that I need a symbiotic joining of my world self and my authentic self to bring the best results, the tension that sometimes emerges between these two gives me the energy to go on.

Today I seek to "own" my real self.

Fifty-three

Illness teaches me that my life is a story of God's fingerprint on me.

Year after year, and day after day, even hour after hour God has always been with me. God has shepherded me through all the sunrises and sunsets of my time on this plane. God has never abandoned me, nor will God ever. How could God abandon me when God's essence is in me, and God's power and might upholds me? God did not make me simply to fling me out into a violent and dangerous universe.

God's fingerprint is on me and it is in this indelible mark of God's love that I find God's presence and wisdom imprinted forever. God gave me identity, a special and authentic identity, which fascinates and delights me. When I take the time, when I become silent and listen to God's voice, the steady middle "C" note of the universe that resonates in my soul, I find myself at peace.

How strange that it was my illness that's provided the new forum for deeper understanding of the mystery of God's total and absolute definition of me—a holy pattern, unlike any other, that has made me into a holy shape recognizable only as God's child.

Today I cherish God's fingerprint on me.

Fifty-four

Illness teaches me to understand the grand design of my life.

I see myself as so clumsy, so insufficient, so lacking in spiritual poise and bearing. I am but a poor substitute or facsimile of what I believe I should be. Yet, at the same time, I know that God did make me special, as special as a leaf on a tree, as purposeful as a thunderstorm, and as necessary as a frozen winter's day.

After all, I know that in God's making I am important. My being here now is part of the grand design of divinity—the intentional pattern of celestial breathing in and breathing out. I'm part of the overall schema of wonder of God's creation. Because I'm part of the grand design, then my life must likewise be an intentional stitch in the cosmic tapestry of love that God is continuously creating all to show the fullness of Love. I'm part of the plan, and perhaps in some strange way even my illness is an element in the plan.

I know without question that God didn't will me to have illness, but I believe that it is God's Will that the spiritual strengths God gave me become more fully activated by my illness, allowing them to pour out their wonder onto a world that so needs healing in all forms: justice, patience, compassion, wisdom, courage, etc., etc., etc.

Today I see God's grand design.

Fifty-five

Illness teaches me to honor the many lessons I have learned over the years.

Every decade of my life, from the formative childhood years (birth to age 10) to the wonder years (80 plus), is packed with lessons upon lessons. Illness has stimulated me to re-view and re-think my life with new eyes of grace.

Illness has given me clearer eyes illuminated and tempered by suffering, and granted new thoughts enlightened by a more accurate assessment of what is real. Illness has awakened my heart and soul to embrace my inner qualities, my spiritual strengths, and to recognize the presence of God in everything I've done over the years, both accomplishments of note, and behaviors of guilt and shame that punctuate and season my life like salt and pepper.

My illness has so accented God's handiwork in and on me; it has helped me throw away any attitudinal antiques that were cluttering my mind. My illness has allowed me to perceive my current life situation more clearly, and to develop a new and authentic meaning of what this life has brought me so far.

Today I honor God's profound presence in me all of my years.

Fifty-six

Illness teaches me to perceive time differently.

Illness has changed the way I perceive and value time. Before my illness I lived in tomorrow. My focus on and interest in today was only relevant so far as it added to tomorrow. I was constantly preparing, preparing, and preparing for something to come. My past was only valuable to the degree that it helped me today to prepare for tomorrow. My internal time clock was stuck on the future. What happened yesterday was a blur for me, hardly recorded in my brain because I was too busy preparing for tomorrow.

I was like a squirrel always gathering acorns for the winter, running and scurrying in hyper-activity. My body lived in today, but my mind rarely did, it was consumed with tomorrow. My concept of "now" was weak and underdeveloped.

Illness has changed all this. I realize that all I have is the "now," the present, moment, only today. In the new "now" of the present I look for the grand presence of God everywhere. I see my world as a diamond now, ever flashing rays of light, lasers of love. In this new today, I see my spiritual strengths sparkle not just in me but everywhere. And I am grateful!

Today I keep today as today, not tomorrow.

Fifty-seven

Illness teaches me to confront the big questions of life.

We confront the questions like *"Who am I?"* and *"What am I supposed to be about now?"* and *"How am I doing in life?"* and *"Where is God?"* at various stages and transitions of life. But for me these questions have never been more plain and palpable than I find them now in my illness time.

The questions seemed to ride in with my illness, galloping right at me like racehorses out of the starting gate. At first they terrified me, fearing I'd be trampled. But eventually I found them gentle and kind, supportive and strong. I rode each one, always coached by my illness to be patient, to listen to the whispers inside me that would give me new direction and new confidence. Now these big questions are my trusted friends, comrades I can rely on.

It's not that I suddenly have all the answers, but my illness has taught me there's something bigger and better than answers. My deepening faith gives me peace and consolation far more than any answer I could ever parse. I don't ask, *"Why am I living?"* anymore. I simply ask for direction about "how" to live the best today.

Today I live the big questions of life with utter confidence.

Fifty-eight

Illness teaches me to seek the newness of life.

As illness shoves me into a new life space, my desire to make clearer sense of my life intensifies. Several internal forces converge creating a tipping point of decision. Do I continue to use the same assumptions and expectations, and the same attitudes and values I always found useful (but that now feel cumbersome), or do I let go and pass the baton of my life direction to a new hand awaiting its arrival?

Illness has raised my awareness of this choice, and has prompted me to pray for the strength to choose the more growthful path. Illness pulls me along so I can discover a fuller newness of living. I find I now live with a new sense of priority—what was formerly important seems less so now, with new priorities emerging to take their place. The shift to newness is at first confusing, then subtle, and gradually becomes more and more pronounced until it fully eclipses what was.

Illness gives me a new depth perception allowing me to better distinguish what makes the most sense now in my life. My spiritual strengths become electrified and begin re-molding my very personality away from the worldly and toward the numinous. My newness is hard to describe, yet boldly prominent in my introspection.

Today I am brand new.

Fifty-nine

Illness teaches me to understand/comprehend the mystery of life and living.

As I look back on my life, a practice certainly accelerated by my illness, I see that my primary aim (without consciously realizing it) was finding the unifying, cohesive, integrating force that holds me all together.

I long for completeness, a sense of wholeness, which renders some form of comprehension of the mystery of life. At one and the same time, my illness both creates new mystery and also provides insight into that mystery. Illness has made me more comfortable with the mystery, with the unknowing.

While illness diminishes me physically, it also, when I let it, gives purpose to my diminishment. The psycho-spiritual effects of my illness on me are in themselves mysterious in that they resist analysis, scrutiny, and measurement. Yet, the effects provide a new synthesis of soul, a new freedom of being, and a new boundless growth potential. I becoming more comfortable with my new mysterious life; it provides a new and curious security of self that was unknown to me before my illness.

Today I flow with the mystery of life.

Sixty

Illness teaches me that a deeper gratitude is at the heart of a successful life.

Illness forces me to confront myself and there discover that my truest identity is spiritual. Things have become all the more real to me since my illness diagnosis.

I look around me and take in the glory of nature. I am genuinely enthralled by nature now in ways so different than before. I find myself bursting with gratitude for the simple things: a leaf, a shade of red, a songbird, a bud, and even a weed that I formerly thought of as an intruder only worthy of destruction, all have now become kindred life friends.

My gratitude extends to people who I now seem to naturally search out for their glory, and beauty, and wonder. I now notice their kindness and truth, compassion and acceptance, faith, and courage rather than the opposite that formerly captured my attention. I find myself being thankful for all sorts of things I previously overlooked.

I've adopted what I can only call a worshipful attitude toward all that is. I am amazed by the semi-sacredness of all things and all truth in people and in me. I marvel at the monumental assistance that God has showered upon me.

Today I am grateful for a grateful heart.

Sixty-one

Illness teaches me that mourning is necessary and positive...it has immense value.

Illness has accelerated my spiritual life in far greater measure than any other event in my life. Illness has brought me face to face with death, and this ultimate human loss has paradoxically multiplied my spiritual depth. This shock of looking death in the face motivated a kind of pre-mourning in me.

This proximity to death did not bring a veil of tears, a depressed affect, or a sorrowful continence; on the contrary this face-off with death, the pre-mourning, has done the opposite. Walking around the edges of my own mourning has only heightened the promise of God's joy and life in abundance—not just in eternity but right now as well.

Mourning holds me up; it provides me a lesson in God-reliance, confidently depending on God's grace and love to provide all I need to deal with the ultimate pain of loss. Mourning doesn't pull me away from God; it pushes me deeper into God and God's spiritual strengths in me.

Today I mourn joyfully.

Sixty-two

Illness teaches me to receive care from others as well as give care to others.

There is a time for every purpose under heaven, a time to give and a time to receive (Ecclesiastes 3:1-8, NIV paraphrased). For so long, I thought that giving was somehow better than receiving. Illness has taught me the folly of this assumption. In God's economy of love, we need both givers and receivers; at different times in our lives we're called to do and to be both.

In a strange way receiving love and care from others is equally holy as giving it. Illness teaches me that it is God's power in balance between the giving and the receiving that gives me the gift of vision I need to appreciate the joys of life, and the strength to deal with its sorrow. Only after I absorbed the spiritual shock waves of my illness diagnosis (with God's grace), could my thinking evolve to realize the symmetrical and symbiotic relationship between giving and receiving.

This revelation led to an even more consoling revelation that my needs provide the opportunity for another person to give love. The inspiration of Love is possible only with the expiration of Love. God's cosmos is breathing Love in and out in perfect balance. Illness mysteriously is part of this balance in which we all take part.

Today I receive and I give.

Sixty-three

Illness teaches me that I cannot honor others by dishonoring myself.

To honor means to give praise and even reverence. To honor means to appreciate and respect, to give title and distinction. Yet, in honoring life, and others, and God I also elevate (honor) myself, and there find inspiration, not diminishment.

I can offer honor in many ways, including growing in obedience. But perhaps the most equitable and loving form of honor in human terms is the notion of "being with" another, of not abandoning them in any way. "Being with" also applies to me. Illness has taught me to be with myself more intimately, to be sensitive to my own needs and not abandon my desires.

Illness offers me no special entitlement, but it does give me permission to "be with" myself and with others in a new and fuller presence. Illness has taught me that I must not abandon myself in body, mind, or spirit. I honor myself, others, and God best by being the full and authentic person that I've been made to be. Illness lets me see my authentic self clearer, and become more intimately engaged with it.

Today I honor all and everything.

Sixty-four

Illness teaches me to better distinguish between my needs and my wants.

I can still hear my mother's words to me when, as a young boy, I would ask for something unnecessary. *"Your wants are many but your needs are few."* she would say to me. These words couldn't be more apt than they are to me today with my illness.

Illness instructs me to draw a finer line between what I simply want, and that which I truly need. I'm learning how to break dependencies developed before my illness. I'm traveling lighter now, trying to move to simplicity of living and conserving my energies for my genuine needs. I'm realizing, fuller and deeper each day, that what I formerly thought of as essentials, actually aren't, and things I thought of as non-essentials are now actually spiritual life necessities.

I'm finding that the intangibles of my life are of paramount importance. I find these the most valuable to blunt the physical discomfort and the emotional distress that visits me often. I'm finding that what I need most is hope, and faith, and courage, and compassion. These powers have taken on a new luster in my life—they are my new needs; without them I would be in torment and constant trial; with them I'm strong and safe.

Today I know my needs.

Sixty-five

Illness teaches me the difference between a "quality" and a "quantity" relationship.

How I now crave the "touch" of a quality relationship, and find myself almost repelled by a "quantity" relationship. The difference between these two relationship conditions is ever more evident now that illness is my traveling companion.

I long for the emotional sharing that defines a relationship as "quality" or genuine and I find the emotional distance and the superficiality of some relationships oh so tedious now. I long for interpersonal connection, a "place" where I can feel comfortable expressing my feelings freely. I like conversations that focus on the mutuality of both of us, the bonds that bind us, and dislike ones that focus almost exclusively on my illness.

I find interchanges that seem only concerned with my medical treatment and the mechanics of living now quite shallow and unsatisfying. I prefer discussing my new interior awareness, new insights, and mental/emotional surprises, rather than food, politics, sports, etc.

I prefer talking about love rather than fear (that seems to be everywhere). I want to talk about real news, not the fear-evoking kind that only parades as news in our media. For me this is where quality touch lies...and I crave it!

Today I crave quality relationships.

Sixty-six

Illness teaches me to go beyond right and wrong.

Through the trauma and triumph of illness, I've learned that my personal attitude about illness colors my entire illness journey. Yet, trying to distinguish between what attitudes are "right" and which ones are "wrong" is not only tiresome but also quite impossible, and perhaps even inconsequential.

Such mental machinations leave me drained and agitated. Illness has wiped away the notion of right answers and wrong answers on many fronts. Right and wrong assumes an outside standard or "should," it assumes there is some judge making the rules and "calling the shots." Such notions seem oddly irrelevant to me now.

Illness pushes me into a world where I'm called to rely on my conscience for guidance. I certainly need an informed conscience, so I gather whatever data I can manage, and I mix it together with my personality strengths and place it on the altar of grace within me, asking the Spirit for guidance. It's only then that I can make an informed decision what is most appropriate for me now. While ethical and moral rights and wrongs are real and helpful, most of the decisions I face are not ethical and moral *per se*, they are human.

Today I ask the Spirit to guide my decisions.

Sixty-seven

Illness teaches me that finding fault is fruitless.

Somehow my illness has made things more real for me. It helps me distinguish what's important and what's simply trivial...one of these is my penchant for finding fault.

In a former career I taught medical interns and residents the soft side of medicine: counseling skills and the like. I remember one physician who couldn't help himself from finding fault. His method or target was different however. Whenever someone died he'd always find some way of faulting the deceased for somehow causing his own death. *"She was overweight!"* *"He didn't exercise enough!"* *"He let himself go!"* were some of his common post-mortem laments. I found this troublesome then, but as I look back on it now I'm merely amused that he needed such rationale. What was he protecting?

But, of course, I do the same thing. I especially do it with my illness. *"What did I do or not do, that gave me this illness?* I ask myself. This illness must be a punishment for some 'sin' of commission or omission! *Where did I stray to deserve this?* All such thinking is fear-based and faultfinding; it's all quite baseless and meaningless. It matters not at all.

Today I am out of the fault-finding business.

Sixty-eight

Illness teaches me that I cannot change anyone.

Before illness I actually thought I could, and perhaps should, change others and myself by my own force of will. I thought that such change was right and necessary, and that I was somehow charged with accomplishing it. I now call such beliefs my "terrorist's beliefs" because they do such wanton damage in an undercover capacity.

Some examples of these include the following: I actually thought that I needed other people's approval. I operated under a "peace at any price" mentality, which only ensured that I remained in turmoil. I thought I needed to be super-responsible to feel worthy. I thought there were things or ways unique to me that only I could help others change. I thought that I was supposed to solve or "fix" any problem that came along. In some strange and certainly erroneous way, I actually thought that I was supposed to "do it all."

Now, with illness as my master teacher, I see so clearly that I was trying to change reality. I was trying to change personalities, shift beliefs, transform thoughts, and otherwise rearrange feelings by myself. I was a hidden critic who was out to change the world. Illness has taught me that change belongs only to God.

Today I realize that only God can change people.

Sixty-nine

Illness teaches me that simple and direct communication is best.

Illness has taught me to be direct, not only with others, but perhaps even more so with myself. Illness increases my self-talk; I'm internally talking to myself more than I ever noticed.

Before my illness I was sloppy in how I related to me, consequently I gave myself erroneous messages and sometimes felt "less than." Now I'm clearer with myself. When I sense a less-than-positive emotion, I immediately stop myself and discern what I've been telling myself that could make me feel so badly. Once I get some notion of how I've been talking to myself I can quite intentionally change my internal message and instead give myself messages of strength, messages straight from my spiritual strengths.

I try to stay in my strong, spiritual center and do my very best to keep out of my shadows and compulsions. Every day I'm getting better at giving myself messages that are most accurate and most real about me—messages from my spiritual center...my spiritual strengths.

Today I enjoy direct communication.

Seventy

Illness teaches me everything and everyone is my teacher.

My illness gives me new eyes, eyes that see the same things and people I always saw, but I now see them differently.

Before illness I had a bad case of "critical eyes." For some unknown reason, I scanned the world for "what was wrong." Seek and you shall find. I found lots of wrong, lots of things that I thought needed fundamental change. Now with illness as my teaching coach, I'm training my eyes, through the power of my perceiving spiritual strength, to see what's "right."

Personality characteristics or behavioral patterns of others that I formerly found noxious (even obnoxious) I now give special attention—not so I can correct them or somehow use as evidence that I'm better than they are, but simply to learn from. I've learned that the personality traits that I want to criticize most are exactly the ones from which I have the most to learn.

My illness has given my eyes a truth-seeking quality and has taken away my faultfinding faculty. I now search for what there is to learn in any situation. I continuously scan my personal horizon, with its people, places, and events, seeking how God is seeing this. Everything and everyone is my teacher now.

Today I have many teachers.

Seventy-one

Illness teaches me that "peace of mind" is my highest human good.

Before my illness I had lots of goals: I wanted to be somebody important, I wanted a comfortable life, I wanted people to like me, and I wanted my wife to love me unconditionally. I wanted status and affirmation (even praise) and appreciation from others. I wanted to be "in the know," to be the sought after "go to" person, and to be seen as competent (smart)—even seen as a paragon of moral and ethical "rightness." With all these wants, it was hard to be happy.

My illness has helped me shift my wants and reduce them until today when I can identify "peace of mind" as my premier desire. My only goal today is to learn how to love better than I did yesterday. The means I use to achieve this solitary goal are the only means at my disposal—my spiritual strengths, all of which come from Love and are unique reflections of Love.

My spiritual strengths are my endorsement from God. Now that my wants are more aligned with truth, I find that the result of this new alignment is peace of mind.

Today I seek only peace of mind.

Seventy-two

Illness teaches me that I am never alone—God is always with me.

It's through my illness that I have learned to relate more intimately with Love (God) itself. When I take the time to look deeply into my eyes in a mirror, the eyes of a person with illness, I see Love. I realize that the reflection I see in those eyes is the image of me as God sees me—an image of Love.

My illness brings me in closer contact with the center of life, the flash of divinity in me, the power and might of the universe, and the epicenter of all energy—God. Whatever the means that brings me all of this, it is holy; it is sacred.

I still can't say that my illness is holy and sacred, but its "fruits" in me certainly are. In some strange way, it is a privilege to have illness as my companion, because from this vantage point I do see glimpses of God where I never saw God before.

I believe that my new status as a person with illness affords me a special grace, or at least accents the grace of my spiritual gifts. The grace gives me the power to plod on along this desert road of illness that offers me so many spiritual oases along the way. It's at this place of spiritual respite that I find refreshment in the pools of clean and clear water that cleanses me of any loneliness.

Today I am never alone.

Seventy-three

Illness teaches me that healing is not the same as curing.

Oh, the energy and the resources, the money and the brain power that our culture expends on seeking cures for all the sicknesses we contact and maladies we incur! We could financially bury ourselves in bankruptcy, and expend all our time and talent looking for that right combination of factors and forces that would eradicate all our physical woes. Might it be possible?

Yet how much of this same finite energy and resources do we use seeking methods for and practicing the art of healing the illnesses that flow from our sicknesses? A sickness is a medical diagnosis; the medical community seeks to cure sickness. Our illness is any of our noxious attitudinal or behavioral consequences of our sickness; we seek to heal illness.

We seek cures for the sickness of any medical diagnosis; and we seek methods for healing the illness of our sicknesses. We need the best of both for either to work optimally.

Today I seek curing and healing.

Seventy-four

Illness teaches me to embrace my own God-given "gifted" personality.

At the core of me is a human operating system, and unlike computer operating systems that are all alike, my operating system is absolutely distinct from the 7 billion+ people who live on this planet. In addition, and even more incredible, my operating system is distinct from any that have ever existed and any that will ever exist on this earth.

This operating system is my personality, that schema or structure of uniqueness that makes me...me! God uses my personality to show Love, all the infinite varieties of Love that there are. Each of us has a unique personality made so by the Love infusion that God has invested in us. My job here on this earth is to express the Love-infusion, this special, one-of-a-kind Love packet of divinity that God has planted in me, as accurately and as completely as possible.

My illness enables me to show more of my particular Love packet more clearly than probably any other experience I've ever had. Illness, by being the threat that it is, draws out my spiritual strengths (and my shadows and compulsions as well) as nothing else can. Illness primes my spiritual pump so I can gush forth the Love of God that dwells within me. I indeed am gifted.

Today I embrace my gifted personality.

Seventy-five

Illness teaches me to become an "exceptional patient."

Oncologist and surgeon, Dr. Bernie Siegel, M.D. working at Yale University Hospital, noticed that about 15% of his cancer patients were different, so different in fact that he dubbed them his "exceptional patients."

In his book, Love, Medicine & Miracles, Dr. Siegel described these exceptional patients as ones who did not see death as the greatest failure of life; rather they saw the greatest failure of life as not living optimally today, regardless of the condition of their body. They saw Love as the primary healing agent that brings total health, and they were less disturbed by the losses that illness brought their way than most other patients.

My research into the reactions of various persons with illness agrees with Dr. Siegel. It told me that indeed there are about 15% of the patient population who do not necessarily react negatively to their illness, but respond to it by tapping into the most powerful healing agents there are—their unique spiritual strengths; this is truly exceptional. I call these patients "spiritually-healing patients."

Today I strive to become a spiritually-healing patient.

Seventy-six

Illness teaches me that Love is the primary power of the universe.

Spiritual power, the power to heal, has many forms all of which are represented as virtues. Yet, across the wide spectrum of spiritual power, illness has taught me to realize that all spiritual healing power is "Love in action."

Love is so gigantic, so immense, and so pervasive that I can't possibly see it directly. I can only catch glimpses of Love when I attune my perception to its presence. I see flashes of Love manifested most accurately in virtue. All virtue is the presence of Universal Love. This Love has already taken up residence in me in a unique way and is the healing power I call upon to bring healing to my illness.

My illness, to quote Dr. Siegel, is *"my opportunity to live as I have never lived before."* To this I would add: *"and to open the gates that have prevented me from fully taking part in God's loving action within me—the primary power of the universe."* All power comes from God. God is holy, indeed the fountain of all holiness, the source of all grace, and the epicenter of all that is real.

Today I am in Love in my spiritual strengths.

Seventy-seven

Illness teaches me to appreciate the value of my shadows.

I am endowed, as we all are, with six spiritual strengths (graces). Each of these six is the premier power of one of the six functions of my personality. These six spiritual strengths provide all the energy necessary for me to be the authentic self that God intends me to be.

Yet, because I've been gifted with these six strengths, I am simultaneously vulnerable to the shadow of each of these six strengths. A shadow is a "place" in me where the power of the strength is absent, the opposite underside of the strength. Illness has taught me to make friends with my shadows rather than trying to wring them out of my personality—which is quite impossible.

My shadows can cause me pain. But if I understand my shadows and observe how they operate in my life, then I can "de-fang" them and actually listen to the clues they offer me as I'm unknowingly moving away from my spiritual strengths; they sound the alarm, so to speak, that I need to return to my Holy Center—my spiritual strengths.

Today I embrace my shadows.

Seventy-eight

Illness teaches me the sacred truth of In medio stat virtus.

Standing straight and tall at the center point of my personality I discover my spiritual strengths. *In medio stat virtus*, is Latin for "in the middle lies the truth (or power, or virtue)."

At my spiritual core, in the center of my personality, I find the true me, the authentic, genuine article of me. I did nothing, and can do nothing, to earn my spiritual strengths; they are truly God's gifts to me. I do not deserve them, I'm unworthy of them, yet God has seen fit to bestow them upon me.

The healing waters of God flow from the center of my personality, which was formerly unknown and unappreciated before my illness. These waters cleanse me, quench my spiritual thirst, and refresh my soul; they prepare me for healing, for transcending my illness and finding new life in the midst of what otherwise is simply pain, punishment, and endless trial.

Today I seek my center, the wellhead of healing power within me.

Seventy-nine

Illness teaches me to embrace my compulsions as instructors of my soul.

If my spiritual strengths are in the middle of my personality, and my six shadows are to one side, what is on the other side of the middle? My compulsions!

Compulsions emerge when I try to use my strengths not for the benefit of others or for any healing, but for my own very human personal aggrandizement. I use them to gain something for myself on the human level. Compulsions then are perversions of my strengths.

The compulsions that flow from my spiritual strengths are presumption, bluntedness, perfectionism, ingratiation, unreality, and arrogance. When I distort or otherwise dismiss my strengths, it's very easy for me to descend into any one (or a combination) of these six compulsions.

Just as my shadows can block healing, so can my compulsions. Yet, like my shadows, compulsions can also be my teachers. If nothing else, compulsions alert me when I'm "off-center." They "tip me off" if I'm awake to them, that I'm about to become spiritually de-stabilized and unbalanced.

Today I embrace my compulsions.

Eighty

Illness teaches me to become more aware of my beliefs as the fundamental assumptions of my mind.

All the beliefs I hold in the believing function of my personality, together form a conception of the world that is absolutely unique to me. This assemblage of beliefs, attitudes, and "knowings" form the undisputed view of reality that is mine alone, and which defines me.

Illness brings me face to face with my beliefs about what "should" be, the way "things should operate," and all my assumptions about what is "right." It goes on to instruct me what needs changing; which beliefs, perceptions, thoughts and feelings need to shift so that I can live more in the center of my soul.

Even my ideas about who I am and what I'm about on this earth needed changing once illness became my companion. I could no longer hold onto beliefs that I was an achiever, an athlete, a counselor, or even an author. All these definitions from the world paled before me as insufficient when illness turned on its scorching spotlight and exposed my real self. Illness demands that I become a more real, more kindly, and more accurate model of the self that is truly me.

Today I'm more aware of my fundamental assumptions.

Eighty-one

Illness teaches me that I am stronger than I am weak.

Illness pushed me off my pedestal of unknowing; it took the blinders from me and shook up my psyche. Illness sent shock waves through me. What remained after all the shaking and tumult were the pillars that God had erected in me at my conception—my spiritual strengths standing like monoliths of power.

When all else had been shaken away, when all that was unnecessary was removed, I could clearly see what was my true success and what was merely for show. I am a success, I am stronger than I am weak; indeed, in my weakness I find my strength (2 Corinthians 12:10, paraphrased).

Illness unfolds the many paradoxes of me: that I must face death before I can live fully; I must give-up so much so I can receive; I must let-go so I can gain a firmer grip; and many more. I am resilient, steadfast, courageous, and strong, much more than I am fragile, unreliable, timid, and weak. I am God's child of power and might.

Today I am success itself.

Eighty-two

Illness teaches me to become more aware of my awareness.

Before illness visited me, I unwittingly had forfeited my own awareness; I let my awareness be captured by all that glittered and flashed, all that the world thought was real, all that seemed to offer fun, excitement, power, money, fame, and success. I wasn't even aware that I had lost sight of my awareness, if I ever had awareness of my awareness at all.

Now, with illness as my new mentor, I look deeper at my awareness. I've awakened to what deserves my primary focus. I see differently; and more than that, I now know that I do have the power to direct my awareness. I've gained new insight and a new outlook; I've developed new spiritual intuition, and a clearer view of my interior authentic self. I realize now that I had scales over my eyes—distorting what I saw and making me stumble about in the dark.

I now see a great light, my illness has pushed me into a spiritual space of bright sunshine where things are made clear, the shadows are revealed as paper tigers, and I am shedding my fears. I'm aware of a new horizon and a new sun that is rising on me. All is blessed! All is Holy!

Today I am aware.

Eighty-three

Illness teaches me to take firmer charge of my thinking.

My thinking was distorted before I was diagnosed with my illness. In so many ways my thoughts were inaccurate, even illusionary. I was so self-referential, so self-focused that I used my thinking function only to bolster the masks I wore, the values I held, and the vision of me and the world that I thought was real.

I developed thoughts based on insufficient data; I polarized my thinking to make my world fit into neat but inaccurate packages of either good or bad; I made judgments about what would happen based on what I wanted; I jumped to the worst conclusions about others; I thought I was being persecuted; I let my feelings direct my thinking; I blamed and labeled; and I put myself on a pedestal. I was functioning in my shadows and compulsions and didn't know it!

It took illness to shake me out of my stupor of unknowing. Now my goal is simply to think accurate thoughts, not necessarily positive thoughts or negative thoughts, but just simply accurate ones.

Today I direct my thinking and not the other way around.

Eighty-four

Illness teaches me to become "in touch" with, and to share my feelings.

Before my illness I just wanted to feel good. I continuously searched my world for what would please me, entertain me, bring me "up," and make me happy. I was emotionally immature and foolish at my core. I let my feelings run my life; they were in control. I had no concept that I could influence my own feelings, that I had power over my feelings and not vice versa. I did all I could to "stuff" any negative feelings, resist them, project them onto others, disguise them, and otherwise push them aside. I was living in an emotional *la la* land.

Now that my illness has taught me that feelings are primarily motivators of decision and action, I strive to be as emotionally honest as possible, with others and myself. I work to specifically identify my feelings; decide if I want them; figure out what thoughts generated them; and determine how to adopt more accurate thoughts and/or take active steps to express my feelings by changing my behaviors.

I know I'll never perfect this new process I've adopted, but illness reminds me often to keep working on it so I can stay in the holy center space of my spiritual strengths as much as possible.

Today I am "in-touch" with my feelings.

Eighty-five

Illness teaches me to live in wholeness.

When I'm whole, I'm more holy, more in touch with the packet of divinity in me. When I'm whole, I'm psychologically integrated, I'm figuratively glued together better, and all my disparate parts begin working together as a unit. When I'm whole I'm undiminished, strong, and constitutionally united. When I'm whole, I experience coherence, a fantastic transcendence of self that allows newness to seep into me and emerge from me.

In the condition of wholeness, I can forgive, I can drop grudges, and I can give up triviality. In wholeness my thinking is expanded and deepened; I discover my many dimensions of goodness; I become unrestricted in thought and limitless in scope; I see the whole, compete picture; and I'm flush with creativity.

Wholeness is a spiritual "high," and illness has brought me to the edges of wholeness. When I catch but glimpses, flashes of wholeness, I am reassured that God is indeed with me. I am blessed—I have seen the Lord.

Today I choose to live in wholeness.

Eighty-six

Illness teaches me to live life as an adventure, not as an avoidance.

One of my favorite psychologists is Abraham Maslow. He is most known for his hierarchy of needs, but another one of his wisdoms is actually my favorite: *"As you travel the road of life and you come to a fork in the road, always take the more risky path, because therein lies the most growth."* (The Third Force: The Psychology of Abraham Maslow, Frank G. Gobel, Pocket Books, 1980, p. 38).

I've never had a more stark personal experience with this quote then when I arrived at the fork in the road known as illness. The initial diagnosis of illness is only the beginning of a string of choices, with each giving new opportunity for avoidance or adventure.

Living a life of avoidance is what the world preaches: insulate yourself against risk; don't take chances; walk the most secure path; etc. Living "avoidance" ensures only one thing...that you will never experience adventure.

Sports psychologists encourage athletes to "play for the fun" of the game—realizing that peak performance is thwarted by playing the game "to avoid losing." And so it is with illness, I've learned to live to the fullest today, to go for the gusto as the old commercial touted.

Today I live the mysterious adventure.

Eighty-seven

Illness teaches me to speak with my real voice.

I always found the statement, *"That person is comfortable in his (her) own skin,"* curious. I didn't fully know what it meant. But now, with illness making a home in my body (but not in my heart, mind, or soul), I need to pay closer attention to my real voice so I can be comfortable in my own skin during my illness journey.

My real, genuine, or true voice is the six voices of my spiritual strengths all aligned into a synthesized and integrated single voice that speaks the clearest wisdom of all. This voice is from the Spirit within me. My job is not simply to find this integration of voice, but also to distinguish my real voice from the other voices in me, the voices of my shadows and/or the voices of my compulsions.

I need to step back from any situation and first remember who I am and perceive the facts objectively yet transpersonally. When I do this I find I'm much better positioned to speak my central truth, speak from my real voice. I'm here in the moment and also in God's moment at the same time; I see both levels of reality operating simultaneously. In this new space, I find I can transcend my shadow and compulsion voices and be real.

Today I listen to my real voice.

Eighty-eight

Illness teaches me to take the risk of action.

An action is a cause set in motion. So what is my cause now that I have illness? What is my most pressing desire now, and what do I need most?

Down deep in the labyrinth of my psyche rests a life purpose that aches to find expression. My cause is but a small, yet very important link in a chain devised and motivated by the Spirit that gives me life in abundance right now. Without this cause, my life is empty, even meaningless. Too many good people with medical diagnoses suffer the added illness of "having no cause."

My illness probes and prods me to discover and clarify my current life cause and put it into action. My cause awakens my soul, stimulates my personality, and brings new meaning to me along with it. This meaning activates my internal healing mechanisms. My cause must be about Love and must involve helping others in some way.

Right at this moment I'm writing this book, which satisfies a cause, but there will come a time when I'll be unable to write. At that time I need to graduate to a new cause—my very presence will then be the occasion for others to show love/care/compassion to me. This new cause will be no less "real and meaningful" then, than writing this book is right now.

Today I take the risk of action.

Eighty-nine

Illness teaches me to honor my internal power of choice.

Every success and every failure begins with a choice, a decision. I think I was a lazy decision maker before illness entered my life; I now need to change this.

In past times I let the situation make choices for me; I would "go with the flow" by sizing up the current facts as I saw them and choosing the least restrictive path. I zigged and zagged through life with an apparently flaccid set of life principles. The principles were there, but for the most part my guiding principles lay limp in my belief core.

Now, with my illness, everything has changed. My principles and attitudes are energized. I'm much more aware that I can make choices based not on the exigencies of the moment, leading to situational decision making, but choices based on what I believe and what I know is right for me. These aren't the easy situational choices I formerly made; rather they can be hard choices that require every bit of the power of my spiritual strengths.

I can't afford to be a lazy decision maker any longer; I must exert holy influence over the situation rather than letting the situation get control over me. I need to choose how I will live and thrive with my illness.

Today I recognize the power of choice.

Ninety

Illness teaches me to find truth, beauty, and goodness each day.

My illness has pushed me over a cliff. Right now I'm free floating. I have a choice to either fall to the ground or to fly. I chose the latter. I spread my spiritual wings and catch the thermal updrafts that exhilarate me, fill me with excitement, and invigorate me. The view from such heights inspires me, enraptures me. I find that flying is fun, but more than fun, flying is wonder-full.

When I worked in the hospital I saw too many patients who had fallen to the ground; they had somehow given up. Their diagnosis and treatment simply became too much for them. They were threatened by their illness, stricken with a psycho-spiritual paralysis, and consequently experienced a morbid dis-spiriting of their soul.

Parts of them, their most important parts, had already died. Their ears had closed, blocking out the music of their soul: their eyes were blurred, preventing them from seeing the grandness of creation; and their touch was blunted, letting in no sense of joy and delight. They hadn't learned from the master teacher of illness; they were mute, and blind, and insensitive to the truth, beauty, and goodness that surrounded them.

Today I live in truth, in beauty, and in goodness.

Ninety-one

Illness teaches me to realize that each day offers something beautiful.

Illness trains my eyes to see the beauty of the "now," and shapes my beliefs to anticipate, even expect, that new beauty is just about to begin. Where is this beauty?

My illness has taught me that where I find beauty is where Love resides; and since I know (more than believe) that Love is everywhere, I know that when and if I look deep enough I shall indeed find beauty.

Each day when I first open my eyes to the light of day, I pause to prepare myself for the awesome beauty that this day will bring. I pray that my eyes will see the fullness of this beauty, my mind will fully appreciate it, and that my feelings will be sensitive and carry this beauty to my heart, I can then choose to let this beauty penetrate to my illness sites and bathe them in their special Love—healing them by sheer power of splendor.

I know that Love is present where I find beauty; Love is the central healing power of the universe. I dearly need healing, so why wouldn't I do all I can to experience beauty every day, every hour, and even every minute?

Today I find beauty everywhere.

Ninety-two

Illness teaches me to live the sure mystery of Love.

I find no surety in this world. I don't say this with chagrin, but with a new faith that has emerged in me since illness has come into my life. It seems to me an objective fact that surety is not of this world.

Scientific analysis and medical "miracles" offer no guarantee of immortality; the only thing they make certain is the end of physical life. This is not a criticism but merely a statement of fact. So where does surety lie?

My Illness tells me that surety lies in the mystery of God. Illness further teaches me that all is mystery; certainly for me now what is most real is mystery. I'm settled with this mystery; I'm comfortable. Today it seems rather arrogant, or at least foolish of me to think that I thought otherwise in my pre-illness days.

Now my vision has been liberated from some illusionary mirage; my thinking is unshackled from the press of having to understand everything. Now I realize that the more I do understand, the more I realize the mystery. This paradox is another truth that illness has taught me. This new vision and new mindset is the result of a gradual unfolding of the power of my spiritual strengths (gifts from God) washing over my personality.

Today I live in the sure mystery of God.

Ninety-three

Illness teaches me to overlook the negative and accentuate the positive.

My Illness has causes me to regard what we call "the news" very differently. Formerly, before illness, I actually believed the news was a compilation of the events of the day. Now I see much of what passes as "the news" to be a litany of negativism.

Illness has taught me to seek the opposite of negative. Negativism assumes that today is "not good" because it doesn't agree with yesterday. Negativism then has a hard time generating anything new, and if there's one thing I know I need now with my illness, it's a new attitude. I need new interpretations of what's most important, what's most real, and what's most holy. I need new emotional responses—not the same tired emotional reactions I used yesterday. I need new choices to motivate and activate new ways of living.

These changes are qualitative; I'm not looking to shift the externals of my life, no; it's all what's inside me that needs changing, what's stirring in the recesses of my personality that needs the new light of my spiritual strengths.

Today I overlook anything negative and only see positive.

Ninety-four

Illness teaches me to value heartache as well as elation.

I'm not any more eager to experience heartache than the next person is, but when my heart aches, when I'm sad, forlorn despondent, chagrined, and even depressed, how am I supposed to act? My illness surly gives me heartache. I mourn the losses that illness brings, the pain and torment that accompany it, yet what am I do?

As St. Paul recommends, I should not cry out pleading with God to save me from this hour...no, he says, it was for this (trial) that I was brought to this hour. I can't change the external reality of this hour in my life; I can't magically cure my brokenness; I can't sweep away the pain; I can't make everybody happy. But I can, when I stand toe-to-toe with this hour, and when I stare eye-to-eye into it, begin the work of changing my reactions to this hour.

Actually, it's not me that changes the hour; all I do is consciously and intentionally invite the Spirit in to ignite the healing power and might of my spiritual strengths, the underserved gifts that God has bestowed on me. Only then can I begin to ease, begin to find solace and peace, relief and refreshment. All this emerges in me gradually, like tiny raindrops that begin the sudden downpour of grace that always comes.

Today I can transform heartache into elation.

Ninety-five

Illness teaches me to see everything as gift.

When I learned from my illness that I needed to shift my view of abundance from seeing only the "good" things that I valued and wanted, and learned to include everything, even things, or events, or relationships, or unsatisfying tasks, etc. that I didn't value or want, was I truly ready to actually live in God's abundance.

Now I'm ready for the next tier of learning—that everything is gift. This second learning tier is harder than the first; it means that I had to transform my vision of "everything" dramatically. This new learning certainly calls me to read or view the news very differently. Could a murder somehow be a gift? How? Could crime, and cheating, and an entire unfair world be a gift? I can't see "gift" in these "wrongs" when I view them singularly of course, but perhaps I can find the "gift" in the way I let all this affect me.

Every crime has a perpetrator, and every abuse has an abuser. How do I regard the perpetrators and the abusers of the world? How does my faith instruct me to regard them? Might the eventual shift in my perception be the gift? Might the fact that I now see everything differently be the gift? It's a new world now for me as I turn my vision around and see what I once rejected in an entirely new way.

Today I see all as gift.

Ninety-six

Illness teaches me to develop the courage to be imperfect.

My Illness poses a most compelling question, *"What elements of my total human and spiritual potential lies fallow, and untapped?"* My answer is, *"Quite a lot!"*

The next step is what takes immense courage for anyone, but especially a person with illness who wants to 'play it safe' (such as myself). That next step starts with another question, *"How can I capture and use a greater portion of the spiritual potential inside me?"* Venturing out to find the answer to this question takes more courage, a new courage to risk great loss, because looking into myself necessarily involves finding areas of imperfection inside.

When my quest leads to discovering my spiritual strengths, I come to realize that on either side of my strengths lay very big imperfections and menacing vulnerabilities. On one side, I discover my shadows; while on the other I find my compulsions. These six shadows and six compulsions force me to face all my imperfections with courage.

But, unless and until I could take this risk, I am left with only a half-baked set of strengths; quite inadequate to achieve the healing I so wish for. Daily I'm still scratching together the courage I need, not by myself, but only through and by the lead of the Spirit who implores me to pray, so I can uncover the healing riches inside me.

Today I embrace my imperfections.

Ninety-seven

Illness teaches me to never be paralyzed by fear.

Perfect love, says Scripture, casts out fear (1 John 4:18). The corollary, of course, is the fear can prevent love from blossoming forth.

Fear, the absence of love, casts a pall around me and renders me lifeless because it cuts off the flow of love (grace) from God to and through me. Fear diverts my spiritual energy away from me—leaving me dispirited and even depressed at times.

When I'm depressed I know that my immune system, my body's primary physical defense against illness, is likewise depressed to the point of being rendered insufficient. When this happens, I'm not only emotionally and psychologically paralyzed...I'm spiritually paralyzed as well. In this spiritually sordid place, I lose my bearings and founder with no rudder, no means of forward thrust, no direction; I'm spiritually becalmed, yet frantically unsettled.

All of my shadows and compulsions bellow and screech at me and I'm rendered immobile, lifeless, scared, and yes...paralyzed. The only antidote is Love, the primal energy of the universe of God, which is in me in the form of my spiritual strengths.

Today I'm freed by Love.

Ninety-eight

Illness teaches me to feed my soul every day by remaining open to grace.

My soul is hungry. It needs sustenance, as does my body, so it can be the strong spiritual epicenter of my being. What feeds my soul best now that I have ventured, quite unintentionally, into the land of illness?

The first course of my spiritual meal is prayer. Prayer reminds me who I am and brings me back to my center point of strengths and grace. My next course is silence. In contemplative silence I taste new food so fine and savory, so delicious and nourishing. My third course is forgiveness, coming to realize that what I thought was an attack, wasn't, and giving up all claim to attack back. The next course that illness teaches me feeds my soul: simplicity, living in the real 'now' where all is an offering and a gift. Simplicity is also beauty, and beauty nourishes my soul with animated reflections of divinity's presence.

Next, I look at my life in gratitude; I'm so taken by the abundance of God that I want to give myself over to God, to merge with God. But then I realize that I am already merged with God, and actually have never left God. I'm home, my illness strangely brings me home, a place so familiar yet so foreign.

Today I am totally open to grace.

Ninety-nine

Illness teaches me that I am not helpless...I am full of hope.

My illness threw me into a cauldron of uncertainty like I've never known before. Everywhere I looked my fearsome shadows saw doubt, lack of confidence, weakness, inevitable loss, fallibility, and insecurity. I felt vulnerable to attack and incapable of defending myself against it. I felt feeble, incompetent, lost, and powerless. I was emotionally bereft, psychologically without resources, and spiritually destitute. I felt no hope whatsoever.

I asked myself where hope resided, where could it be found? The answer was simple: hope resides in God alone. Hope provides absolute assurance that God's power and might, unlike human power, cannot be eclipsed; that God's power of Love will always prevail because there is nothing stronger than Love.

I needed to shift my view of hope from a transitory human desire to a rock-solid, God-driven reality. Hope calls me to my center; it pulls me away from disappointment, disillusionment, and eventually from despair, and sets me up in a secure, impregnable place of knowing where my true self resides, a fortress of confidence and strength unlike any other. My spiritual strengths are my weapons that are ever ready. Illness calls me to live in this place of certainty, the center point of love within me, where fear is no longer found.

Today I am full of hope.

One Hundred

Illness teaches me to adopt an internal attitude of a smile.

I now smile a lot. I know that may seem strange since I have illness, but it's true. Illness has taught me to smile. Smiling is the natural response to recognizing the many, many gifts that illness brings me.

Smiling in turn allows me to appreciate my spiritual strengths even more than before. Smiling gives me a positive outlook. On a physical level I just know that smiling strengthens my immune system, it increases my tolerance of pain and frustration. Smiling lowers my stress and blood pressure, and heightens my creativity. Smiling does all this and much more.

As I walk in the land of illness, I always try to wear a smile on my face. This smile is not fake or contrived; it's real, genuine, and grand, and it gives me so much in return. Smiling attracts others, frowning does the opposite. Smiling lifts my mood and relieves my stress; smiling releases natural pain killers in me so I'm more comfortable; smiling helps me stay positive and steadfast in the face of illness when other forces in me push me to run away.

Smiling keeps me sane, sustains my soul, and draws me closer to God. Smiling renders me the genuine truth of who I am at my core—a child of God.

Today I wear a smile.

One Hundred & One

Illness teaches me to luxuriate in the presence of God.

How contradictory it seems, but certainly true, that my illness has brought me full circle, from the depth of near despair to the heights of joy of living and loving.

I find myself ever inspired now, so much more than ever before. I feel that I am infused by the light and life of God's presence in my spiritual strengths. I now see a new reality formerly hidden from me before my illness. My blindedness is now illuminated. It's almost as though I can touch a new reality that exists now (and always has) in me, and all around me.

Part of this new reality includes the mighty mechanisms of healing and care that reside deep within my soul and which I can now coax out into the open. I now see the healing wonders that my spiritual strengths bring to me.

In a hundred and one ways I'm ever drawn to God's mercy and compassion, God's steadfastness and courage, God's inspiration and truth. I do luxuriate in all of this; I stand in wonder, awe, and delight in the practical healing I receive every day.

Today I luxuriate in God.

Postscript: Healing

Healing means change. The primary site of change is my personality, specifically the six functions of my personality: believing, perceiving, thinking, feeling, deciding, and acting. The reason that healing opens me up is because it causes a shift in the way I use the tool of my personality.

Here's a little poem-like piece that helps me remember that I am about change always; when I stop changing, I stop healing.

When I always believe what I've always believed, then I'll always perceive what I always perceived, and...

When I always perceive what I've always perceived, then I'll always think what I always thought, and...

When I always think what I've always thought, then I'll always feel what I've always felt, and...

When I always feel what I've always felt, then I'll always decide what I've always decided, and...

When I always decide what I've always decided, then I'll always do what I always done, and...

When I always do what I've always done, then I'll always be what I've always been, and...I'll never heal!

Thank you and God bless you,

R. P. Johnson

Made in the USA
Lexington, KY
25 October 2014